Rhett,

God Bless ya!

John

John Morgan's impersonation of President George W. Bush is so spot-on that he even fooled the CIA, who started taking orders from John. Wonderfully funny yet respectful of the forty-third president, John Morgan has entertained millions, but there is a message in his madness, and he captures it in his book *War on Fear*. From the time we're tots, we face fears—fears of storms, the dark, and the "boogeyman." While we may get over the fear of imaginary monsters, other fears linger. With authenticity and candor, John shares his own journey from fear to courage to action. With his own flaming sword, John lights our way out of the dark.

—MIKE HUCKABEE
Former Governor and 2016 Presidential candidate

I absolutely love this book! It contains funny, honest, and transparent encouragement. It is full of excellent personal examples and well-placed quotes, and I found myself wanting to quote it and share those quotes with others. I was genuinely inspired, laughed out loud, and even cried as I heard John testify to God's trustworthiness and glorious plan for our lives.

—DANNY JONES
Founding Sr. Pastor (Ret.), Metro Life Church

This book is a sparkling gem. If each of us could trade our fears for courage and peace of heart, it would be worth a million bucks. In *War on Fear*, John Morgan paves the way to make that very trade. Take hold of this gift and don't let go.

—RON FORSETH
Vice President, Outreach Media

WAR ON FEAR

JOHN MORGAN

with **Joel Balin**

CREATION HOUSE

War on Fear by John Morgan with Joel Balin
Published by Creation House
A Charisma Media Company
600 Rinehart Road
Lake Mary, Florida 32746
www.charismamedia.com

Unless otherwise noted, all Scripture quotations are from the New King James Version of the Bible. Copyright © 1979, 1980, 1982 by Thomas Nelson, Inc., publishers. Used by permission.

Scripture quotations marked NIV are from the Holy Bible, New International Version of the Bible. Copyright © 1973, 1978, 1984, 2011 by Biblica, Inc. Used by permission.

Scripture quotations marked ESV are from the Holy Bible, English Standard Version, Copyright © 2001 by Crossway Bibles, a division of Good News Publishers. Used by permission.

Scripture quotations marked NLT are from the Holy Bible, New Living Translation, copyright © 2007. Used by permission of Tyndale House Publishers, Inc., Wheaton, IL 60189. All rights reserved.

Scripture quotations marked AMP are from the Amplified Bible. Old Testament copyright © 1965, 1987 by the Zondervan Corporation. The Amplified New Testament copyright © 1954, 1958, 1987 by the Lockman Foundation. Used by permission.

Scripture quotations marked NASU are from the New American Standard Bible–Updated Edition, Copyright © 1960, 1962, 1963, 1968, 1971, 1972, 1973, 1975, 1977, 1995 by The Lockman Foundation. Used by permission. (www.Lockman.org)

Cover design by Bill Johnson

Visit the author's website: www.JohnCMorgan.com and www.WarOnFearBook.com

Library of Congress Control Number: 2016953793
International Standard Book Number: 978-1-62998-572-5
E-book International Standard Book Number: 978-1-62998-573-2

While the author has made every effort to provide accurate telephone numbers and Internet addresses at the time of publication, neither the publisher nor the author assumes any responsibility for errors or for changes that occur after publication.

Names and details of some stories have been changed, and any similarity between the names and stories of individuals described in this book to individuals known to readers is purely coincidental.

First edition

16 17 18 19 20 — 9 8 7 6 5 4 3 2 1
Printed in Canada

To my bride, Kathy.

You gave yourself to me.

What courage.

Contents

Foreword

The first time I met John Morgan I was backstage on our Duck Commander Cruise a couple of years back, and we were about to entertain our first audience. Half of the ship was excited about what we were going to offer them. When John walked in backstage with that dark suit, a white shirt with a red power tie, and that crooked grin, he *was* George W. Bush! It was so surreal, and you couldn't help but think that you were with the POTUS. We were going to play a joke on Uncle Si and let him think the real President Bush was a surprise guest on our cruise but decided that poor man has suffered enough just being Uncle Si.

John was hilarious onstage in our bit and helped us put on a fabulous and funny show. In between shows, when we were eating backstage with him and his wife, Kathy, is where I really began to see John as who he is and not just as W's impersonator. We all shared a lot of our testimonies with each other, and a bond was formed. When people are not stingy with the victories of God, they make a lot of deep, meaningful relationships and friendships. That's the way my wife, Lisa, and I felt about John and Kathy, and we barely knew them. After the second show John offered to lead some worship at my devotional the next morning, and being that he offered looking like the former president, I said, "Yeah, that would work—George Bush singing gospel songs!" I thought he was joking, and he said, "Al, I am on a praise band and lead worship sometimes at my church back in Florida." I had no idea!

When he came the next morning in shorts and sandals and without his "work clothes," he just looked like one of the cruise passengers. My devotional was as packed as the shows the night before, and this was 7:30 in the morning on a cruise ship! John played his guitar, led us in a few songs, and sang one he had written, and I can't tell you how grand and inspiring it was for me that morning to teach God's Word with the Spirit already moving so powerfully. I realized right then that John was a special vessel for our Lord to accomplish much for the kingdom. He is a great entertainer but an even better person and leader for Christ.

I love this book about the war on fear. John takes so many of the common things we fear and gives us great help in not only overcoming these enemies but actually taking them and using them to gain strength and help others. I've certainly known my share of fears through the years and still bend to many instead of declaring war on them.

When I was twenty-two years old I was called to ministry and recruited by some godly men that I very much respected, but I let fear of the unknown keep me from enrolling in seminary. I was married with two baby girls, and I feared being able to support them. I also thought seminary students were weird, and I feared looking like an uncool nerd—and I couldn't have that! On and on I listened to the whispers of fear and didn't listen to God's call. After a miserable year of not finding success in what I thought I should be doing I revisited my decision. At twenty-three I prayed for God to help me overcome my fears, and I waded into ministry. Including my training, I spent twenty-four amazing years in full-time work, all at my home church in West Monroe, Louisiana. God so richly blessed my life because I let Him guide me through the many fears that came with working with and later pastoring a large church that helped raise me. God allowed me to be a prophet *with* honor in his hometown.

Ironically, when I was faced with a decision to leave my job as a pastor to join our family's show, *Duck Dynasty*, and return to Duck Commander, can you guess what paralyzed me? You got it. Fear! *What if I don't like it? What if I don't have what it takes to be on the show? What happens when the show ends? Will I still be able to do ministry and help other people?* On and on, the fearful questions kept me from making the move that I knew was the right one to make, and so for a year I agonized about getting *out* of full-time ministry. *Déjà vu*, anyone? You'd think I would look back and remember that I had been there and done that, but that's the thing with fear; it's always lurking to take away your confidence and your trust in God's ability to see you through. I finally trusted God and, with the help of some great friends, made the move, and now my ministry has expanded to worldwide opportunities! Once again, fears are defeated when the Lord is trusted and the enemy is engaged.

One of the best parts of traveling around the world speaking now is that Lisa and I get to meet so many fellow warriors for God out on the road. John and Kathy Morgan are two such warriors. John has a natural gift to look like George W. Bush and deliver great comedy to entertain, but he has a more amazing spiritual gift to encourage, strengthen, and help guide others to some pretty amazing grace. When I think about his witness I think about what another John (the Apostle) said in Revelation 12:11: you overcome the evil one by the blood of the Lamb, the word of your testimony, and by not loving this life so much that you would shrink back from death. In other words, you overcome Satan by overcoming fear!

I hope this book blesses you as much as it blessed me. I can tell you that if you follow John's guide to overcoming fear and put into practice his very practical advice you will be a more confident and positive person, and you will be victorious in your war on fear.

—ALAN ROBERTSON
Author, Pastor, Family member
and Star of *Duck Dynasty*

Preface

The photo on the cover of this book is of my son Christopher's brother-in-law Zach. A few months ago Zach was suddenly plunged into kidney failure, hooked up to dialysis, and in desperate need of a new kidney. My Chris donated his own kidney to Zach, and the two of them have been adventuring since.

Zach has had a fear of heights, so this pic marks a significant accomplishment in his life—now that he is still alive. Way to go, Chris and Zach, for not letting fear stop you from adventuring. My prayer is that this book will lead you to many new adventures in a life free from fear!

Acknowledgments

I'm so grateful for my courageous wife, Kathy, who accompanies me around the globe like it's no big deal, loves me and our children like there's no tomorrow, and tells me honestly what she thinks.

To Joel Balin, my great friend and writing partner for this book—Joel, your patience with me is profound, and I am beyond grateful. I'm really, really grateful.

Pam Wisner, your persistent coaching and direction are what brought me out of limbo on this project, and your project leadership was perfect. Kudos on finding the cover pic!

Atalie Anderson, your leadership has taken the project to the finish line on time! You should run for president!

Amanda Quain—Friend, not only are you a great editor; you are a great friend. Your enthusiasm for the content is a great inspiration to me.

Bill Johnson, you are a great graphic artist! Once again you created a masterpiece!

Laura Bowman, your editing chops are great. Thanks for everything you did to help this book be something I am proud of.

Dimitreus Castro, you took a picture and created a work of art. Thank you!

Dr. Steve Greene, your leadership is getting this message into the ears and hearts of people everywhere!

Stephen Strang, your belief in me has made all this possible.

Last but most, I thank You, Lord, with all my heart!

Introduction

Everything you want is on the other side of fear.

—JACK CANFIELD[1]

Don't be afraid.

—LUKE 12:32, NLT

What if? What if everyone could achieve their highest potential? What if fear was a tool to be harnessed and used rather than an overlord keeping us all in bondage?

Could we all be filled with joy, growing, changing, adapting, inventing? Growth is natural. Fear inhibits growth. Its effect on our lives has cost this world great benefit.

What if spring never sprang, birds never sang, eagles never flew? What if fear held in check every speck of color from our world? What we would miss in the absence of this, this kiss, this bliss?

What would we be missing if the Wright brothers never flew? If Edison had given up? If Armstrong had chosen fear rather than to take that giant leap for mankind and land us on the moon?

We benefit from the bold and the daring. Yet still we sigh. Alone in the prison of our own personal fear, we regret. How much we've missed. How much the world has gone without. Not because we couldn't, but because we were afraid.

Fear is trusting in the wrong thing.

I hear a new song rising up. I see a new day approaching, a new way. A fresh new boldness that says, "Let's do this. Let's go there."

Enough of this beige life of blending in. This doesn't look like God's intention. He didn't create birds so they wouldn't fly. He didn't create the sun not to shine or flowers not to bloom or man not to thrive. We are made to *rock this life*, not cower in the corner!

> # We are made to *rock this life*, not cower in the corner!

Men, rise up! Women, stand up! Let's defeat this clear and present enemy called fear and come to bask in that for which we were created.

This book was written to rile you up, to provoke you to anger against the fear that has robbed us and robs from us every day. It's the same fear that robs our loved ones too.

Let me just ask you this one question: Were you created to rise to your God-given potential and maximize the life He put within you? If so, let us accept His gracious, adventurous invitation rather than choose the safety of the bland.

Come on, friend! Enough! The world is missing your contribution. How fun the journey of breaking free! How high the thrill!

Let's go to war—together!

Do you try to ignore your fears?

Do you try not to rouse them, hoping for peace?

How sad to miss much that you could accomplish. Fear takes its own prisoners. I was one of them. For the majority of my young life I let fear keep me, own me. I dreamed of doing. I dreamed of becoming. Do you?

Each decision affects your future, and this moment can change everything. You are one of the heroes, but at the moment you may be a POF (prisoner of fear). You're called to influence those around you. Seeds of world-changing greatness are within you. Conquering fear is vital for fulfilling your purpose, achieving your dreams.

I knew a guy who worked in a wholesale warehouse who discovered a bump on his head. He was so afraid it was cancer that he wouldn't go to the doctor to get it checked out. Over time I watched it get bigger and bigger. Sadly, fear claimed his life. Fear is expensive. It will cost you.

Courage is to dare in the face of risk, from small gestures of love toward a neighbor to launching that business venture you've dreamed of for years.

How much is fear holding you back? Ten percent or 90 percent?

Fear is false! Worry is a waste. How much time do we waste fretting, then find that the task was much easier than we feared it would be. I have said it myself: "That was easy." All that needless dread.

Fear owned me. It dictated my choices. Finally, I got really angry. Now I'm fighting back. I'm doing battle against a soul-sucking enemy and loving every minute of it.

Friend, come with me on this journey, grabbing the adventure you were created for! I'm having a blast fighting fear in my life, routing out an enemy bent on my destruction. I want to equip you step by step, weapon by weapon, to defeat fear as well. With God's help you can rise up and become who you were created to be and do what you were created to do.

It's time to join the battle. It's time to joyfully fight and win the war on fear.

CHAPTER 1

What Is Fear?

Life is an occasion. Rise to it.
—EDWARD MAGORIUM,
MR. MAGORIUM'S WONDER EMPORIUM[1]

I am on a quest to serve by leading people into a successful life on the other side of their fears. I know as a comedian and an actor who portrays George W. Bush I'm supposed to be a funny guy all the time. Fear tells me if I take a somewhat serious role in part of my public life it will dilute my brand, cut into my business.

You know what? Fear can go jump in a tub with a toaster! *Tzzztttt!* Fear is not the boss of me! Well, not most of the time. Is fear the boss of you? Does fear tell you what you can and cannot do, attempting to keep you from the inspiring ambition of your heart? Of course it does. I don't know about you, but that really ticks me off. I don't want fear dictating to me what I can't do with my life, and I don't want it leading you around by the nose either.

The way fear works is that it projects worst-case scenarios in order to immobilize us.

Fear has a useful function to be sure; it can keep us from danger and at times wisely advise us. Good fear can keep us from falling off a cliff, but bad fear might keep us from climbing a mountain.

> **Good fear can keep us from falling off a cliff, but bad fear might keep us from climbing a mountain.**

We need to be retrained in order to make fear our servant rather than allowing fear to make or keep us cowardly, timid, and unwilling to act when courage would step forward.

If you have purchased this book and are reading these words for the first time, *congratulations!* You've taken a giant step toward overcoming the fears that have kept you prisoner! I encourage you to grow angry with me at the fears that have kept you from your lifelong dreams for too many years. Imagine living the dreams in your heart!

You are marvelously designed with creative abilities and have the potential to make this world a better place. But fear can squash your creativity or argue against your daring objectives.

Fear says, "Nah, you don't want to do that. You'll be better off playing it safe. Besides, what if…?"

Fear is not your friend, though it acts that way. He snuggles up to you, puts his arm around your shoulder, and whispers in your ear like he's your best friend. Do you know what I mean? Fear-filled thoughts pose as your advocate, a comforting companion protecting you from the big, bad dangers outside.

Hogwash!

Fear wants to kill you deader than a one-star movie!

Obeying your fears is kind of like scratching an itch. It feels good to scratch, but the more you do, the more it itches. If you keep obeying the impulse you're going to wind up with a hole in your body.

I believe you will thoroughly enjoy the adventure awaiting you in these pages. Hey, you're going to do something with your one and only life. You're either going to sit and waste it, or you can engage and maximize your potential. I encourage you to read this book like it's your own personal manifesto against the rule fear has had in your life, your own Declaration of Independence. Within these pages you will find your armored tank, your rifle, and your battle gear. You will be equipped for the battle.

US President Franklin Delano Roosevelt uttered that famous line, which is often attributed to Winston Churchill, "The only thing we have to fear is fear itself." I think he uttered it when trying to work up the nerve to ask Eleanor out on their first date. I know what the President was talking about. Some thoughts can send my mind reeling. Just fear alone is a great killer of motivation.

At age ninety-two, my dad, who is now in heaven, was occasionally hounded by different fear-filled thoughts. One day, inexplicably, he was deathly afraid to stand up. He didn't think his feet would hold him, so he just would not try. He was terrified. And guess what? Though he was perfectly capable of walking, his feet did not hold him because he simply would not try. Do you see? Fear confirmed. He didn't think he could walk, so he wouldn't; therefore, he couldn't. See how fear alone, though a phantom, can rule our lives?

Do you fear getting old? Dying? Flying? Falling? Clowns? Spiders?

Let me get real. I fear not living up to what I believe is a calling on my life. I fear not being faithful to my bride of thirty-four years. I have asked God repeatedly to kill me (not kill me repeatedly) if I ever get close to being unfaithful to her because I fear her disappointment more than I fear death (I think).

The truth of the matter is, like it or not, fear is at war with us already.

> # The truth of the matter is, like it or not, fear is at war with us already.

An enemy conquered does not have to be reconquered but only kept in a cage, kept in submission. Are you fear's conquered enemy? How do you feel about that? Exactly! Me too. It makes me angry!

Fear can be as silly as being afraid you'll pee your pants on stage. Trust me, from experience, I know that's not the end of the world. (Clean up on stage left!) When I was in the third grade I was assigned the lead in our class play. I was St. George, the dragon slayer. Sometimes fear is as scary as a dragon. But the fire is no more real than a cardboard cutout flame.

With God's help you can slay your own dragons! You can overcome those enemies of your success!

Once I totally froze on stage in front of about six hundred teens. I wanted the stage to swell up and swallow me. Another time I totally forgot my lines right before I went onstage in front of ten thousand people. Horrifying! Fear dictated that I never try that again.

But I'm still an entertainer, a comedian, and a communicator. If I can bounce back from that then you can accomplish your dreams too.

In the midst of really tough times, the apostle Paul chose courage instead of fear. He was imprisoned multiple times, beaten over and over, left for dead, yet he pressed on, because the task at hand was worth the risk. From prison he instructed the Philippian church to rejoice regardless of their circumstances! In the New Testament book bearing his name, the apostle James instructed the church to "count it all joy" when you encounter turbulence in life (James 1:2). Trials and difficulties have a purpose—but it is not to make you afraid.

So why call the book *War on Fear*?

First of all, the name has echoes of the War on Terror. Terror is an extreme form of fear, or the word for "extreme fear." And the word *war* reminds us that this is indeed a fight. The War on Terror is external; the War on Fear is internal. It's personal. It's not so much out there as it is in my head and heart and soul. There is good fighting. There is fun fighting! However, this fighting takes place in our mind, in our thoughts, in our heart, and in our will. After all, since fear gets its foothold through thoughts, the victory begins with correcting untrue thoughts that present themselves as true.

Fear is an invisible but real enemy, and this is an invisible but real war against an insidious foe! It is not an allegory. If you doubt the genuineness and reality of fear, just look at its effect in your life and the lives of everyone you know. Fear is universal. It affects everybody. You can't see the wind but you know it exists by its effect. This invisible wind ends lives and blows down cities. Fear ends lives and careers. It stops forward progress. Fear has a goal, and it's not in your favor.

What relationships were never formed because a young man with sweaty palms and pounding heart just couldn't work up the nerve to ask the girl of his dreams for a date? Fearful thoughts, threats, and projected negative consequences convinced him not to take the risk. And so, no budding love, no young marriage, no grandchildren, and so on. Think of all the missed diaper sales!

How many great ideas, dreams, and visions just never got acted upon because the dream-killer mercilessly smothered that vision and snatched it away before it ever had a chance to breathe or see the light of day?

The thief comes to kill.

I hate fear. I do. I hate it! I hate the damage fear does, and I have chosen to do something about it. This book is my war manual against fear. It's my battle cry, my call to arms.

As I survey the landscape of my years on this planet I cringe at how many of those years were spent in fear. I wonder what cumulative effect fear has had on me, what effect fear has had on you, on the whole human race. But the past is over; we are about to do something that will change your present and future!

Through the truth presented in this book, you can live with less fear—fearless, less and less influenced and tricked by the con artist of fear. Imagine saying from your heart, "I'm not afraid," or at the very least, "I'm victorious over fear, and absolutely anything I need to do—with God's help—I'm going to do."

Cape on!

I'm not a psychologist; I have no PhD. I am just a communicator with a message, and I'm all-in to serve you. I'm *over* being victimized by fear. I've studied this subject, and with God's help, I am winning the war in my own life. This book is me fighting back! It's me fighting for you! I can't fight your battles for you, but I can give you the strategies I use daily to slay my dragons. You have an important role to play. You have to pick up your sword. You have to take action. It starts with the decision to engage in the battle. You are cordially entreated to join me in this epic battle to obtain that for which we were created: our maximized life.

The war fear has waged against you began years ago. Now it's time to fight back, regain your lost ground, and attain the victory! Your victory! Your plunder! Your destiny! Are you in?

When circumstances forced him to answer that question aboard United Airlines Flight 93 on September 11, 2001, Todd M. Beamer saved countless lives when he stared fear in the face and made "Let's roll!" his battle cry against the enemy. Will you make it yours today?

CHAPTER 2

Dominated by Fear

One of my favorite Bible verses is in the Gospel of John chapter 10. In the passage Jesus has been talking about Himself as the Great Shepherd. "My sheep know my voice," He says (v. 14, author's paraphrase). Then He goes on to deliver this very instructive declaration: "The thief comes only to steal and kill and destroy. I came that they might have life, and have it abundantly!" (v.10, author's paraphrase).

Fear is an enemy, a thief, bent on stealing the dreams in our heart, killing the passion we have to make a difference in our world, and destroying our relationship with God and each other. But we are not left defenseless against this intruder. Not by any means.

I know the voice of fear all too well. It has advised me all of my life. An uninvited coach, a counselor of cowardice, a mentor of mediocrity.

Here's how it destroyed what otherwise would have most likely been a glorious moment in my high school years.

I love acting. I have loved it as long as I can remember. My aunt tells the story of the time my family visited New York City. Aunt Claudia took us to see the play *Hello Dolly!* on Broadway. I said to her, "I want to go up there! I want to go up there!" She thought I meant backstage to meet the actors, but I meant on stage. I was all of about eight years old.

In high school most of my best friends were in the drama club with me. We went to conventions together and generally had a blast. This was for me the best part of high school. Even though I dared to get up on stage and act during our school plays, I always took safe, unchallenging roles with only a few lines. Fear never allowed me to try out for a major role. "If you already know you're a failure, why get on the stage and prove it to everyone?" fear of rejection said. "If you get up there and bomb, everyone will know what a loser you really are."

So it was the spring of 1974, the day of the auditions for our senior class play, *1984*, by George Orwell. I had my small role all picked out for the play, one that required little work on my part and one I felt completely comfortable with. As our drama club teacher, Mrs. Jones, started the audition, she announced that she wasn't going to audition for the lead in the play; she was going to award it. She said someone in the drama club had been a faithful member for many years and was deserving of the part. I began to think about the guys in the club. Who would it be? I looked around the room at the different members of the club trying to guess.

"I'm giving the role to—" and then she said it—"John Morgan," she enthusiastically announced. I went into a flushed shock! Everyone else erupted in cheers, nodding their approval. I was flabbergasted, speechless, terrified! I felt like a spotlight was suddenly turned on me. I must've turned fifteen shades of red. I enjoyed the love and cheers, but I couldn't really accept them because my fear of rejection was right there saying, "They're cheering because they don't really know you." I thanked everybody. The next day, out of fear, I made up some lame excuse and quit the drama club.

I want to acknowledge my drama club teacher/coach from 1974, Cheryl Jones, because she took a chance on me. She believed in me even when I did not. I'm so sorry I let her down, but her belief in me planted a seed of possibility that is now growing into its own fruit-bearing tree. Thank you, Ms. Jones! I feel the same sense of gratitude toward my third-grade teacher, Miss O'Brien, for taking a chance on me. Those who pull forward the gifting of others are great influencers. My sixth-grade teacher Mrs. Krehl was another dear soul who pulled me toward my gifting. How grateful I am.

Now I treasure the chance to speak to students of all ages — from grammar and middle schools to universities — to tell my story and empower individuals to be ready when opportunity presents itself unexpectedly, lest fear win another victory.

How many times has opportunity come across your path, only to find you afraid and unable to step up to the plate? How many victories never came about because you and I never even picked up the bat to take a swing?

> ## It's time to take back our birthright,
> ## a life where fear is a conquered foe.

I want to encourage you. It's time to take back our birthright, a life where fear is a conquered foe. The only one that says you have to obey fear is fear itself! The Bible says just the opposite. The phrases "fear not" or "do not be afraid" are all over the Scriptures! When you have God on your side, and Jesus is with you, fear doesn't stand a chance! It's time to take back all that the thief has stolen from us! Game on!

⸻

It all started one day while I was singing.

"On Christ the solid rock I stand..." Words and melody were coming out of my mouth, but my mind was on my discontentment. I was thinking about my life.

It was the Sunday gathering at Metro Life Church, where my family and I have been members for over thirty years. "Why is my life so different from the life I always dreamed I would live?" I wondered.

Not that I was complaining, Thanks to the mercy of God I've been faithfully married to the same lovely girl for thirty-four years. We have four awesome sons and five delightful grandchildren. I've spoken before millions of folks from all over the world and had the privilege of influence. I have the joy of astonishing and amazing audiences worldwide and receiving thousands of rave comments and reviews. I've received letters from folks who have told me that what I shared with them changed their lives.

But still, that day, I thought about how I fall far short of the life described in the pages of the Bible, a life filled with glorious exploits. Anger grew inside me as I realized the power of unbelief and how it has kept me from pursuing and taking action on many of my dreams.

Suddenly my inner anger burst out into a glorious declaration.

"I declare war on unbelief!"

I said it right out loud, said it loud and proud. I declared it boldly and with resolve. I said it out of frustration, out of hating the sinful part of my life, and out of a determination to engage in the battle.

I remember that moment like it was yesterday. I remember where I was sitting. I remember how I felt. It was like the atmosphere around me changed the instant I made that declaration. I felt like

I was knighted and anointed to engage in this age-old battle with unbelief. And it changed everything!

I began to fight against the unbelief I had previously considered normal. Choosing unbelief should never be considered normal or OK. I began fighting my own internal arguments with faith. My heart was made stronger as I decided to be obedient to God and to my own dreams rather than listen to my own radically unbelieving internal dialogue.

Not long after I recognized that fear also was talking to me, advising me, uninvited. Fear played a major role in holding me back from pursuing all that was in my heart, all I was called to do. And so, likewise, I made a bold declaration and engaged in this current battle.

Actually—and I remember this like it happened yesterday—I was alone in my own home when I realized this and boldly and loudly declared, "I declare war on fear!"

And that is what started it all. Now, as I have gained significant advantage over the fear that held me for so long, my heart has turned to those who are, as I was, prisoners of fear in various degrees.

This war goes on to this very day, and I fight this enemy that lives in my heart with unrelenting resolve. But, also, I fight a happy fight. I fight with joy as my strength, joy in knowing I'm defeating my enemy and God's.

CHAPTER 3

The Dream Killer

Recently I was in Minot, North Dakota, for a performance at the grand opening of a new hotel. As a Florida boy, it was great to be in the frosty north. While I was there one evening I thought about how cool it would be to see the Northern Lights. Someone told me they had seen them around 3:00 a.m. several nights before. I stayed awake so I could experience this phenomenon firsthand. I walked out the rear door of the hotel into a desolate and dark parking lot around 2:30 in the morning. It was still a construction area for the tasks yet to be completed at the brand-new hotel.

In the parking lot were leftover construction materials, and I had to carefully navigate my way. As I stumbled through the rebar and scaffolding, behind the parking lot was a huge mound of construction dirt. I stepped hesitatingly into the tall grass behind the dirt mound that blocked any remaining light coming from the hotel. The thrill of seeing the Northern Lights in pitch blackness gripped me as I stared expectantly at the spectacular, starry heavens, awaiting the display.

To my left I heard something moving in the grass. Then it snarled. As I looked toward the sound, fear shot through me like a lightning bolt. The crazed wolf lunged from the underbrush like a sprung catapult, right at me, angry and hungry. As quickly as I saw his angry face, he was on me. I tried to decide between fight or flight, but there was no time. I tried to kick him in the teeth as he lunged at me, but I missed. He sank his fangs into my thigh, and I screamed in pain as I wrestled with him, grabbing a clump of fur and trying to pry his mouth off my leg and beat on him. I finally got away long enough to land a good kick, which sent him scurrying back into the darkness while I hobbled my way back to the hotel as fast as I could, clothes torn and bloody, tripping on bags of concrete and iron beams.

OK, OK, so the wolf part of my story was only imagined, but the fear I felt chased me out of the field nonetheless. A totally imagined scenario played like a movie in my mind, causing me to flee, to actually run from nothing. I felt so stupid—safe, but stupid. In that moment I preferred safe. That imagined fear short-circuited my chance at a once-in-a-lifetime opportunity.

Fears are often like that. You consider a choice or path and suddenly you see a dark film play out in your mind, but it's usually a worst-case scenario designed to stop your best intentions.

The job promotion, the big sales call, the offer of a movie role, the invitation to speak, the nerve to ask the girl of your dreams to the prom, the opportunity to share your faith, go on a dangerous mission trip—these and myriad other scenarios are the battleground of fear. It is here that fear waits in stealth for just the right moment to attack. Like a crazed wolf, fear stalks with just the right message to produce the scenario of doom, whose design is your defeat.

You'll fail. You'll be rejected. You have no talent. You'll look stupid. She hates you. You'll be eaten by cannibals. (That one still scares me.)

Fear's goal is to end any forward movement you were making or even contemplating. It curbs your enthusiasm and stops you dead in your tracks.

> Fear's goal is to end any forward movement you were making or even contemplating.

Miraculous Turnaround

Immobilized, I sat on the couch, not knowing what to do and afraid to try anything. My phone simply quit ringing, and the money dried up, but not the bills. Quiet panic gripped my heart, and I was stuck. My mind and body were frozen in a fear-filled quandary.

It's not that I was unaware that a new president might change things for me. It was just that I am an eternal optimist, and I just foolishly assumed that things would simply work themselves out, that I would just know what to do when the time came. Kathy called it denial. However, the time actually did come. We didn't just get a new president; we also suffered a powerful recession. These were two crushing blows to my career as an impersonator of a now former president.

George W. Bush impersonators were just not on anybody's radar anymore, and I was scared senseless that I would never be hired again. The obvious thing would be for me to go back to the appliance business that I left for this new career as an impersonator, but inwardly I just knew I wasn't supposed to go back. I knew I had to move forward, but I just didn't know how to proceed. I was too scared to try anything. I prayed a lot during that time asking God to help me. This is how He did.

I got a call from the owner of Mardel Christian Bookstores. He asked me to come to Oklahoma City to speak at a manager's meeting. I checked my calendar, and the date they asked for was open. Of course, at this point all my dates were open. I quickly said yes. Then I thought, "What am I going to say to a group of working managers with actual jobs when I can't even manage my own career?" But there was an honorarium I couldn't pass up. "Fake it till you make it," I thought, but I was inwardly afraid that I wouldn't make it at all. It took all the courage I could muster just to go.

I began to do some research into the company to prepare for my keynote to the managers. What I found out astounded me. First of all, then-CEO Mart Green had just donated over $70 million to Oral Roberts University to pay off all of their past debt. OK, that's impressive. His leadership saved the financially troubled institution. Mart's billionaire father, David Green, is the founder and owner of Hobby Lobby, the chain of over four hundred craft stores that employ over twenty thousand people. Green is very generous and has done very much to get the Bible translated into many languages and distributed worldwide.

As I was researching all this I randomly (or so it seemed at the time) came across a clip from a movie called *Facing the Giants*. It was an inspiring scene about a football player who had already given up on believing his team could win their upcoming game. His coach helped him to discover that he was capable of far more than he thought. I watched the clip—because I'm too easily distracted—and went on with my prep.

When I arrived at the expansive headquarters shared by both Mardel and Hobby Lobby I was taken by the warm and beautiful surroundings. I was impressed when the receptionist greeted me by name when I entered the lobby. The Hobby Lobby lobby. This was no doubt a company with an appreciation for their guests and an appreciation for beauty.

I had a very positive experience with the great folks from Mardel. They were gracious, and everyone enjoyed our time together. I had agreed to visit a few of their stores to do book signings. One of them was in Tulsa. The manager asked me to pick something from the store as a thank you gift. Glancing around, I saw a book called *Facing Your Giants* by Max Lucado. It reminded me of the movie clip I had seen, and I also thought, "I'm facing my own giant right now."

That night I read a good portion of the book, which is based on the famous biblical story of David and Goliath. Lucado points out that the future King David, at this point still a shepherd boy, had spent much time in the presence of God marveling at His majesty in creation and experiencing His power to deliver him from harm. David was close to God and altogether aware of God's overwhelming preeminence above any enemy. So when he became aware of the Philistine giant Goliath taunting the army of God's people, David didn't see the problem with earthbound eyes; he saw it as though from God's perspective. God holds the nations in the palm of His hand. Goliath was like a grain of sand compared to Him. David went forth confident not in his own strength but in God's. In case you don't know the story, David tried on the king's armor, but it was too heavy, since he was only a boy. He had no choice but to walk into the battle without armor and armed only with a small sling. He selected five smooth stones from a stream, and with the first one in his sling he killed the mighty giant.

I began to see that I was looking at my "giant" problem from a couch perspective. I needed to see it from God's perspective. Indeed, I didn't need to keep staring at the problem at all. When we stare at our fears, giving ear to their poisonous proposals, we give them credence and we easily believe the lies. The longer we listen to them, the stronger their influence over us grows. When we place our trust in and put our focus on God and His powerful intention for us, the giants become defeatable. I began to feel a bit of hope as I read. I began breathing easier.

> When we place our trust in and put our
> focus on God and His powerful intention
> for us, the giants become defeatable.

That night, back at my hotel, I checked my e-mail and noticed an invitation to a book release party in Tulsa for the new Daniel King book. Daniel is an evangelist I have been following for years because of his bold goal to reach millions of people with the gospel, yet he is under thirty years old. Although I had to fight through my fear and intimidation, I sensed this could be a God moment, so I found his number and called him. I told him I was a fan and was in town, and he said, "Sure, c'mon to the party."

The party was on a wonderful but very snowy Saturday night. Someone at the party invited me to attend Victory Christian Center the next morning, where the late Billy Joe Daugherty was pastor. I was excited to go.

Check this out! God was setting me up for a major intervention! Pastor Billy Joe preached an amazing sermon called "Don't Give Up."[1] I don't know what prompted Mart Green to invite me to Mardel or why I just happened to be there when Daniel King was hosting a party or why someone invited me to VCC the next day. But I know I was supposed to be there because the sermon I experienced at VCC turned my life around and gave me the perspective I needed to know that I was right where I needed to be.

Right from the very beginning of the sermon through to the very end, it was like Billy Joe was talking directly to me: "Whatever you're going through, whatever you're facing, don't quit. Don't give up." Billy Joe preached about the apostle Paul on that ill-fated ship bound for Tarshish. It was tossed about for days on end, the sky so dark that they couldn't tell if it was day or night, until finally, as it says in the Book of Acts, they all gave up any hope of living. That's when God spoke to Paul and told him that no one would lose his or her life. God will allow tests to come into our lives, but our job is to keep on trusting, hoping, praying, and doing.

Then after Billy Joe had almost finished this inspiring sermon, speaking directly into my weary heart and instilling hope and faith, he brought an example to the people, a visual aid to drive the point home: the movie clip from the film *Facing the Giants*. Yes, the exact same clip I thought I had randomly seen on my computer days earlier, which led to me choosing the Max Lucado book of a similar title. Then there was the e-mail, the e-mail that told me about Daniel King's book signing in Tulsa, where I was invited to attend this life-changing sermon. When I saw that clip come up on the big screen, I knew. I knew God orchestrated bringing me here and was talking directly to me. He was telling me to face my fear with truth, to believe what God said, not what fear was dishing out. To believe that with God's help I would be able to do all that He has called me to. God had brought me halfway across the country to make sure that I knew that it wasn't over; I wasn't over. God had me right where He wanted me, facing these exact challenges, which I would overcome with His help.

But He knew something I couldn't have known at that point. You, dear reader, are part of this story. God had you in mind when He revived me from my depressed, doubtful heart, for you can now hear the same words: don't quit. God isn't finished with you. It's not over. You can make it over the goal line. There's more for you to do.

God isn't finished with you. It's not over.
You can make it over the goal line.
There's more for you to do.

I didn't know it then, but Billy Joe Daugherty had terminal cancer when he preached that sermon, and he died not many months later, on November 22, 2009. He lived until he died. His words live on in the hearts of all who were ever inspired by his ministry. And now I pass that message along to you. Fight the good fight until you reach the finish line, when every effort taken for His glory will be rewarded.

> *I do not consider myself yet to have taken hold of it. But one thing I do: Forgetting what is behind and straining toward what is ahead, I press on toward the goal to win the prize for which God has called me heavenward in Christ Jesus.*
> —PHILIPPIANS 3:13–14, NIV

CHAPTER 4

The Nature of Fear

The only thing we have to fear is fear itself—nameless, unreasoning, unjustified terror which paralyzes needed efforts to convert retreat into advance.
—FRANKLIN D. ROOSEVELT,
FIRST INAUGURAL ADDRESS, MARCH 4, 1933

To define fear is to defang the wolf.
—JOHN MORGAN, JUST NOW.
FANGS YOU VERY MUCH!

Fear is a distressing emotion aroused by impending danger, evil, pain, etc., whether the threat is real or imagined. It is an unpleasant, often strong emotion caused by anticipation or awareness of danger.

Fear is often an indicator of the way we should run, but we too often run in retreat when what we should do is actually advance. If a fear's intention is to prohibit our best course, as it so often is, then it indicates we need to move forward and do it in the face of the emotion of fear.

Panic in Atlanta

My fears were telling me that I would fail. I wanted to run and hide, cower in the corner. I had been invited to entertain on the Sean Hannity Freedom tour. Well almost. I was actually hired to perform one night in Atlanta in front of ten thousand fans on the tour to "see how it goes." If I did well, I would be on the entire tour. If not... *Fear*. I would be humiliated, fired before I started, blackballed from any important tours in the future, and bushwhacked! The result was stage fright. Five minutes before I was to speak, my mind went blank. I couldn't think of a single line in my script. In fact, it was very hard to think at all. It was like my mind froze. Panic set in.

From within I heard the accusing voice of fear: "You idiot! Why did you take this job? Now you're going to make a fool of yourself in front of ten thousand George W. Bush fans! Your career is probably over." Adrenaline was coursing through me like a fire hose, my blood pressure was mounting, and fight or flight was fully engaged. Then I heard another voice: "Trust me."

Right in the midst of my panic I felt a surprising, calming peace. I remembered that God is faithful and that He is for me and for all these people. I remembered the many biblical stories of God's unfailing help for those who trusted Him, and His admonition, "Do not be afraid." I remembered my own numerous experiences of His faithfulness.

Even though I felt this assurance, my brain was still on lockdown. My manager, Vince, showed me the script to refresh my memory, but the plain English words looked like Greek to me, and I definitely don't speak Greek. I told him I could barely remember my own name. He asked me what I was going to do.

I said, "I'm going to pray, trust God, and head up onto that stage." Vince said, "Are you sure?"

"I've never seen Him fail. God is going to help me now," I replied. Somehow in spite of my panicked heart I knew it would be OK.

My entrance music, "Hail to the Chief," started playing. I knew I had just a few seconds left. I began walking toward the steps leading up to the gallows, I mean, the stage. Ten thousand excited fans were waiting to see why they were hearing that song and there was still no script recall. About two steps up it was like God changed the controls in my brain from freak to think. As I finally ascended the last five steps up to the stage, it all suddenly came flooding back. Rather than what moments ago felt like a certain disaster it actually turned out to be one of my best performances ever. Whew! Thank God!

> *I sought the LORD, and He heard me, And delivered me from all my fears.*
> —PSALM 34:4

So, what was that all about?

American neuroscientist Joseph E. LeDoux, who does primary research on brain mechanisms related to emotion, fear, and anxiety, calls experiences similar to mine the low road and high road responses to fright.[1] The low road, which caused my brain freeze, is mediated by the amygdala, which creates a reactionary, unconscious, rapid response to threats. But there is also the high road, which in my case enabled me to push past fear and its debilitating effects. Neurologically, the high road is a thoughtful, reasonable response that is handled by the sensory thalamus and enables us to process with our cortex, or thinking part of the brain. This part is just physiology, folks.

However, these reactions and responses can also be empowered by spiritual forces as well. Following just the low road and giving in to initial fears, when repeated over and over again, creates a stronghold. A stronghold is a deeply embedded thought pattern that attempts to keep you from the path God has for you. Think of it this way: it's like a furrow or a groove in your brain that sends thoughts habitually down a harmful path.

The good news is that along with these low roads and strongholds there is the high road. Spiritually, rather than our thoughts being led down a stronghold's groove, we can fill in the stronghold's ditch with the truth of God.

But the truth only helps you if you know the truth. That's why the psalmist said, "I have hidden your word in my heart..." (Ps. 119:11, NIV), and Jesus said, "You will know the truth, and the truth will set you free" (John 8:32, NIV). Rather than being a prisoner to fear or the emotions it causes, we can be free.

> # The truth only helps you if you know the truth.

Earlier in my life I had strongholds of fear that hijacked my thoughts. They stopped me dead in my tracks or sent me down the wrong path. But by the time I had my brain freeze experience, I had learned to trust God, stand on His Word, and face fear head-on.

Imagine if we were all courageous enough to act on our best thoughts instead of our fearful ones. Imagine how many Goliath-sized strongholds would be toppled if we acted in faith using truth as a weapon. Put that in your sling and fling it.

Fear makes the wolf bigger than he is.
—GERMAN PROVERB

Truth conquers fear.
—JOHN, THE DRAGON SLAYER

On one level, fear is an impersonal, purely chemical process in the brain that automatically triggers freeze, fight, or flight responses whenever the brain senses a threat. This automatic response occurs in all animals and is the Creator's great gift to His creation to help us survive.

In a scientific experiment mice were conditioned to fear a certain loud noise by receiving an electric shock every time the noise was played.[2] Soon the mice became afraid of the noise because they anticipated the shock whenever they heard it. When the noise would sound, they would have an expected physical reaction, tensing up, anticipating the shock. (I had a teacher in grammar school that affected me the same way.) Even after the shock was removed the little mice still showed immense fear whenever they heard the sound. A stronghold had been created. However, as the sound was repeated over and over without the accompanying shock, the mice eventually began to fear the sound less and less, until over time they seemed to normalize.

The way I overcame the fears that paralyzed my life and continue the process of overcoming fear is to confront the thought I am being presented with and consciously replace it with a truth-based thought. I challenge the incorrect future scenario being presented to my mind with forceful replacement, thus retraining my brain to think more courageously. Repeating this procedure as often as the fear presents itself causes the power of truth to overcome the power of the perceived fear.

This has had a tremendously positive impact on my ability to take action, as I have confronted fear after fear and replaced it with courage. Let me be the first one to tell you that I have not yet arrived, but conquering fear is a fulfilling adventure, and the outcome is a life lived with greater meaning and purpose.

What If...

There was a time in my life when just the thought of trying to form new friendships would trigger the pain of past failures and the fear of rejection. This would effectively shut me down, like the mice cowering under the anticipation of pain because of the memory of past shocks.

Fear plays movies. It plays with your mind. It paints a picture of doom and gloom and terrorizes you into avoiding the thing you actually want to do. What if...

What if I fail? *(Done that.)*

What if I forget my lines? *(Done that.)*

What if I get booed off the stage on national TV? *(Done that.)*

What if I'm disliked? *(Done that.)*

What if I'm hated? *(Done that.)*

What if she rejects me? *(Done that.)*

What if I can't accomplish that goal? *(Done that.)*

What if I miss the deadline? *(Done that.)*

What if I show up late? *(Done that.)*

What if I break a guitar string? *(Done that.)*

What if I forget my zipper? *(Done that repeatedly.)*

What if I pee my pants on stage? *(Done that too!)*

Sheesh! I could wonder how I have the guts to get out of bed.

The potential scenarios are endless, but the point is this: fear argues with your dreams. Fear argues with your ambition. Fear argues with your goals. If fear wins, you lose. So do all those you might impact.

You can train your heart to recognize these productivity-robbing "what ifs" and stop them before they get a foothold in your thoughts. The easiest and most important time to throw fear out of your mind is *now!* The minute you sense it, deal with it before it creates a stronghold. Think of fear as a fast-growing weed that seeks to entwine itself around your will. Pluck it quickly! Pluck early, pluck often.

CHAPTER 5

Fear of Terror

June 12, 2016. Terror came to America's backyard in Orlando, Florida! Forty-nine people were killed and fifty wounded. It always happens someplace else till it comes knocking at your city. Orlando is my town, my stomping ground. It's where I live, my birthplace. I get the season passes to Disney and Universal Studios. I was born in the very hospital where they brought the victims. My first address was Church Street, and I grew up in the inner city. I've driven past the Pulse nightclub where the attack took place many, many times.

Weeks and months after the attack, Orlando is still in the conversations and prayers of people around the world. As a speaker I travel quite often. It was strange seeing Orlando all over the news in city after city, around the world. People in Orlando are living in fear, and because of this calculated attack people everywhere are more fearful.

Now, of course since then there has begun a rash of heinous crimes around the world, causing fear to explode as dear folks fear for their very way of life.

The night before the most deadly terrorist attack on American soil since 9/11, right down the street, in my town, there was a sweet, young female singer named Christina Grimmie gunned down as she greeted fans right after her concert. My pastor and some of my friends were in that parking lot when the shooting occurred.

Orlando has been dubbed The City Beautiful. Ironically, a few months earlier, Europe's most beautiful city, the City of Love, the City of Lights, in a moment became one of the darkest, most terrifying cities in the world. Eight terrorists suddenly and methodically opened fire and set off suicide bombs in various locations in Paris. It resulted in over one hundred and thirty people getting killed and many more injured.

These were horrible acts of violence against peaceful people just living their lives. The news media jumped into fear-mongering action. They know fear sells. If you, dear reader, are among those struggling to find peace in the midst of this storm, you are not alone.

You are not alone. Those may be some of the most comforting words I can tell you during a time of such uncertainty.

I have been encouraging our police officers, other first responders, and our troops for many years. They need our love and gratitude now more than ever. I sympathize with the families I know with loved ones serving in the military, or the families of police officers. God bless you, and may His Spirit comfort you and hold you close and give you peace in the storm.

When I began writing this book the headlines were dominated by news of a shooting in Oregon in which Christians were specifically targeted for execution; one in San Bernardino, which until the Pulse massacre was the worst terrorist attack on American soil since

September 11, 2001; and the Paris bombing, all of which happened in late 2015. This chapter has been amended and updated many times since then as new, terrifying episodes have sprung onto the scene almost faster than I can keep up with them.

Like 9/11 years ago, these events impose a new level of fear and anxiety. It no longer seems feasible to believe that anyone is actually safe. Yet, I believe we can all live well above the fear that terrorism imposes, at peace amidst the storm. Whether you live in Yemen or Yellowstone, Baghdad or Boston, peace is available to you even in the midst of acts that create an environment designed to produce crippling fear and rob you of peace.

Consider the meaning of the word *terrorism*: "the systematic use of terror, especially as a means of coercion."[1] That is what the enemies of our country and the enemy of our souls do. They use fear to coerce us into shrinking back, becoming ineffective and unproductive. Ultimately their goal is that we give in to their demands and give ourselves over to their control.

"Sure," you might think, "that's easy for you to say. It's one thing to just blurt that out. It's quite another to live it out." True; I would agree. We cannot experience the grace provided for another person in need, only for ourselves. I have experienced a home invasion, and my sister had a brick thrown through her window during race riots, an incident from which she and her boyfriend narrowly escaped, though they were briefly hospitalized. I don't know what it's like to be shot at or to watch my home be threatened by fire or a flood. I cannot know what an experience is like until it is upon me. Therefore I pray for future grace to be with me in the time I might need it.[2]

> ## I pray for future grace to be with me in the time I might need it.

The knowledge of truth and a relationship with the Prince of peace, which leads to actual peace in the midst of trials and the personal storms of life, is powerful whatever the occasion of its necessity.

Joel Balin, who helped me write this book, and his wife, Trace, were on a flight that had just taken off the runway when they heard a loud explosion. The plane shook, stopped its ascent, and felt like it was stalling. Immediate thoughts of a terrible crash and the end of their lives came to their minds. As they clasped each other's hands and said a quick prayer, they both noticed an unmistakable wave of deep peace. The peace didn't make sense as the plane limped forward, heading back toward the airport while seemingly losing altitude. Yet, that peace remained even during the shaky landing. As they exited the plane the gray-faced pilot told them that had the engine exploded twenty seconds earlier they would have crashed.

What could explain such peace? Joel assured me that he is not prone to that level of courage. But the Bible tells us that God is "an ever-present help in trouble" (Ps. 46:1, NIV). Sometimes it's hard to trust in the faithfulness of scriptures until we experience them. This was a clear case demonstrating that "the peace of God, which surpasses all understanding, will guard your hearts and your minds through Christ Jesus" (Phil. 4:7).

The Morning of 9/11

It was a beautiful, sunny Tuesday morning in Orlando. I was in business with my mom and dad, running our new-and-used-appliance store. I was alone on a delivery. I turned on the radio in our Ford pickup when I heard, "Two planes have crashed into the towers of the World Trade Center in New York City in an apparent terrorist attack on our country."

I whipped the truck to the side of the road, mouth open. A thousand questions flooded my mind. Senses heightened, I strained to hear the announcer on the radio, though his voice was perfectly clear.

> ## I strained to hear the announcer on the radio, though his voice was perfectly clear.

"We just got a report that apparently another plane has crashed into the Pentagon. America is under attack," the news anchor said, his voice unsteady.

I slammed my transmission into drive and rushed to my delivery location, hoping that there would be a television. It was an apartment complex, and I quickly joined the manager, who was already glued to her TV. That's where I and most of America stayed for the next sixteen weeks—filled with fear, glued to the TV, radio, any news outlet we could find.

In the midst of all this the anthrax attacks began. Someone was sending the lethal bacteria that causes the disease anthrax through the mail. The Capitol Building had to be evacuated repeatedly. A south Florida newspaper was attacked. I remember thinking, "No one is safe." That thought opened the door in me to levels of fear I had never experienced. During those awful, seemingly endless days, I often found myself shivering, though I wasn't cold. I normally sleep like a baby, but sleep evaded me. It was hard to eat. I lay awake night after night and worried day after day, unable to get my mind off of my apprehension.

It's amazing how diabolically far fearful thoughts will take you if you give yourself over to them.

> ## It's amazing how diabolically far fearful thoughts will take you if you give yourself over to them.

It seemed during those dark days that fear had a death grip on all of us. We were glued to CNN, Fox News, and other outlets, as we were starving for more information. But what really were we doing watching all the shows? We were feeding our hungry fears.

If you're old enough, surely you remember your own trauma during that awful day and the following season of uncertainty in 2001. Many of those fears were confirmed. We went to war. Many mothers' sons and daughters gave their lives during those conflicts. Sadly, nearly three thousand people lost their lives on that tragic day in September alone. I cannot begin to understand the horrors those victims and survivors experienced. Perhaps some of you reading this today are dealing with post-traumatic stress disorder because of the events of that day. New York City's finest ran toward the danger and saved many lives that day. The stories of heroism and courage are inspiring. And of course, the War on Terror continues, even to this day.

I remember how calming it was to hear President Bush give relevant addresses during those days. It gave me such hope to know that he was on the job as Commander-in-Chief and that he was not denying, not politicizing, not minimizing this event. He was crying with the hurting while leading our nation to respond properly to this clear and present danger. The President threw out the first pitch in game three of the World Series at Yankee Stadium in New York City. Saturday Night Live came on, and we did our best not to let fear win. We grieved those who died, we comforted those who suffered loss, and we, as a nation, moved forward. We did not cower to terror; we rose to the challenge.

The month following 9/11 I attended a conference. Christian author and speaker Terry Virgo came to America from the United Kingdom and delivered a message that changed everything for me.[3] First, he reminded us that we were not alone. He said that folks from all around the world were praying for America at that time. That brought great comfort to my anxious heart.

He also reminded us that the testings of this world can make us stronger. He shared examples of God's faithful care throughout history and that He is an ever-present help in time of need. He shared that God is ultimately in control even when circumstances make it appear that He is anything but in control. I was reminded that God has a plan for my good, and that I can confidently place all of my trust in Him regarding my past, present, and future.

> **God is ultimately in control even when circumstances make it appear that He is anything but in control.**

I realized that I had stopped trusting God as I once had and had replaced a peaceful heart with an anxious, worrisome one. I recalled God's care over my life all my years and His faithfulness to me. I realized that though circumstances had changed, God hadn't. His promises to help us through every storm were all I needed. Through prayer, I asked Him to forgive me for allowing fear to have such a place in my heart, and I placed my trust back in Him.

I have said these things to you, that in me you may have peace. In the world you will have tribulation. But take heart; I have overcome the world.
—JOHN 16:33, ESV

September 11, 2001, didn't take God by surprise, nor did it move Him from His position of omniscience, omnipresence, or omnipotence. As fear takes over our imagination, it attacks the truth that God is able to protect us from harm and to give us power to handle even our most difficult situations.

Fear internalized grows in power over us, and our sense of safety shrinks. As we agree with fear, it's like we are saying it's true. Fear plays movies in our head of imagined outcomes of worst-case scenarios that are not true. The design of fear is to rob us of courage and to stop us in our tracks, even cause us to retreat. That was what the enemy of America intended to do; that is also what the enemy of our souls intends to do. That is one reason we should not give in to fear.

Terry's message that day was a timely reminder of truths that gave me the strength I needed to put everything back in its rightful place. I remembered that though people, circumstances, and even I had failed, God had never failed, and He has always been trustworthy and faithful. That reminder served as a powerful weapon against the lying, intimidating, internal voice of fear.

One of the mightiest weapons in our arsenal against fear is remembrance, remembrance of God's faithfulness. God knows that we tend to forget, plus we tend to listen to the latest dreadful news. Fear is rude. It is not passive; it is aggressive. Fear tries to make us forget the truth of God's trustworthiness.

King David, a man who had faced as much fear and terror as anyone, said this in response to those attacks:

I will remember the deeds of the LORD; yes, I will remember your miracles of long ago. I will consider all your works and meditate on all your mighty deeds.

In this quote from Psalm 77:11–12 (NIV), David remembers how he faced lions and bears that came to attack the sheep he was shepherding, how he was saved over and over, and that recollection gave him the confidence that God would not abandon him in his time of need. He told himself to take courage and remember all God had done for him.

David remembered, "The LORD, who rescued me from the paw of the lion and from the paw of the bear, He will deliver me from the hand of this Philistine!" (1 Sam. 17:37).

Fear of terrorism is like a taunting, Goliath-sized giant. It intimidates us. It tells us how small and helpless we are. But with God's help we can rise up like David and stand in the peace of the Lord and defeat the fear that keeps us immobilized.

You may think that you are merely an ordinary person who is helpless, but remember that David was still a young shepherd boy when he slew Goliath. Courage to overcome fear comes to ordinary people with faith in an extraordinary God.

I place Scripture passages and courageous or encouraging quotes on index cards, sticky notes, and refrigerator magnets and put them around my house so that I have easy and regular access to their messages. We will become what we believe, what we say, what we think about. The importance of making sure we are feeding into our lives a steady diet of Scripture, encouragement, and courageous motivation cannot be overstated.

We act out of our beliefs. The enemy knows this. During World War II the combatants dropped thousands of leaflets to tell their enemies that the fight against them was futile and hopeless and that they should just give up. Terrorists do the same thing today with videos and social media. The news and Internet sites cooperate by distributing these fear-filled messages and images. The enemy of our souls does the same thing. He will parade thoughts and images of fear across our minds. Fear to go to a public event, fear for our families, or fear to travel can keep us immobilized.

To protect ourselves from this terror tactic, we need to combat the fear-filled and fear-inducing stimulus and media and instead fill our lives with the kinds of examples and beliefs we want to emulate. God has provided us with many ways to move from fearful to faithful.

> ## God has provided us with many ways to move from fearful to faithful.

The Bible says to "fix your thoughts on what is true, and honorable, and right, and pure, and lovely, and admirable. Think about things that are excellent and worthy of praise" (Phil. 4:8, NLT). The following verse says to "practice these things, and the God of peace will be with you" (v. 9, ESV).

Whoever will feed us will lead us. It will inform what we think, how we feel, and how we act. If you feed and dwell on the ways of God and His provision, protection, and grace, you will live out of that input.

I love a scene from the movie *The Hiding Place*, which is based on the book of the same title. It is the true story of Corrie ten Boom from Holland. Her Christian family hid Jews from the Nazis in their home during World War II. She and her sister eventually wind up in a concentration camp. In the scene, she is facing what seems like certain death, and a memory is brought to her mind. She is a small girl being tucked into bed by her loving father. She says, "Papa, what is it like to die?"

Her tender, thoughtful father says, "Do you know, when we go to Amsterdam, when do I give you your ticket?"

"Right before I get on the train," Corey answers.

"Right," affirms her Papa. "In the same way, when the time comes, your wise and loving heavenly Father will give you all the strength you need."

If we put all of our hope and trust in our heavenly Father, in spite of the fact that terrorizing things do happen, we can live in the very real truth that our loving Father cares for us and watches over us. The peace that passes understanding is available. That peace came by the grace of God through Jesus to people living in perilous times.

It is just as available, just as powerful, and just as comforting today because that peace is found in the Prince of peace himself.

Safe in the Arms of Jesus

I was working for my mom and dad on April 19, 1995, when a truck bomb was detonated outside the Alfred P. Murrah Federal Building in Oklahoma City, killing one hundred and sixty-eight people and injuring more than six hundred. I remember that the incident sent fear through my dad, who was confronted with this new thought: "No one is safe. I'm not safe."

That new fear drove my dad to ask me to tell him more about my relationship with God. Dad had always been the self-proclaimed "sane one" in the family. That was his excuse for not giving his life wholeheartedly to God. That day his happy-go-lucky, every-day's-the-same world came to a startling halt. He was afraid. If they could do that in Oklahoma City, the heartland of America, they could do it anywhere. He needed a greater hope, a deeper trust.

I had the extreme honor of sharing my faith with my dad, and after a long, thoughtful conversation I prayed with him to make a full dedication of his life to God. That day my father received what the Bible calls a peace that passes understanding. He fell in love with Jesus and lived out the rest of his happy life with a new joy and deep peace that only increased until the day he met his Savior face to face.

Dear friends, God is love. He is all-knowing and all-powerful. Do you think God is afraid? Of course not. Then let us snuggle up to our Daddy, our Papa, our heavenly Father, and reside forever in His wonderful, protective care. He will never leave us or forsake us.

CHAPTER 6

Fear of Insignificance

For you formed my inward parts; you knit me together in my mother's womb. I praise you because I am fearfully and wonderfully made.

—PSALM 139:13–14, NIV

Our worth isn't created or measured by what people think about our physical appearance, things we do, or even who we are. We have worth because God loves us.

—ROBERT S. MCGEE[1]

Why am I here? Who am I? What gives my life meaning on this spinning, blue ball? Out of the 7–plus billion people living on the earth, do I really matter?

You matter. You count. You are noticed. You are loved. Really?

Personal identity, it is said, is divided into three parts. Who you see yourself to be, who others see you to be, and who you really are. But, there is a fourth reality—how God sees you.

Bullying has always been a problem in our schools. Many kids fall victim to those who find their own place by dominating others through intimidation and violence. Bullying impacted my identity in a profound way as a youngster.

I was a happy and sensitive kid as I entered school at age five. I was a goofball who loved to have fun and laughed easily. I was not gifted, however, with a sense of what was appropriate, and I often got into trouble, both with the teachers and the other kids. My memory of those years is dim, but I know I was obnoxious. Because of this, and because I was tenderhearted and cried easily, I was the favorite target for the mean kids at school.

I learned very early in life what rejection feels like. I learned what inner hurt and wounding from taunting and teasing felt like. I was looking forward to making new friends, being happy. Yeah. Not so much.

I went from being comfortable and carefree to feeling alone, like a nobody, and I was treated like I was worthless. My new reality was shocking. I became afraid and quiet because I didn't want to say something stupid that would lead to more rejection. I hid my situation from my parents, because like so many who define their own identity based on what their peers say, I believed what the other kids said. As I wondered what was wrong with me, I didn't want my mom and dad to find out what a loser their only son really was. I was hated and told so. I hid in the shadows for years, afraid that people would discover my (perceived) true worthlessness.

Over time I learned just to shut down my emotions. I had been taunted for crying so many times I just shut it off. I couldn't feel the hate anymore. The problem was, I couldn't feel love either. I felt completely insignificant. By the time I got to high school I had established a fake identity and hid my true self from everyone to avoid the rejection I knew would come if people knew the real me.

One of the ways I fed my need for significance was to connect with important people and impressive things. It's not surprising. We are wired to be associated with something and someone significant. It makes us feel important ourselves. We seek to acquire things and associations considered important—designer clothes, the coolest cars, and the coolest people—in order for others to perceive us as significant.

In my twenties I traveled as an inspirational singer/songwriter. I loved the stage partially because I truly loved helping people but also because I was silently saying, "Look at me! Give me your attention so I can feel important." We all want our lives to count. We want to know that our existence is valid and that we are loved and worthy of love. We will often hitch our wagon to whatever provides this feeling of validation, even if it's temporary or just an illusion.

I idolized my music heroes, whose rock-star status gave me something to get excited about. On February 9, 1964, when I was eight years old, I watched The Beatles on *The Ed Sullivan Show*. I was fascinated and bewildered by the degree of Beatlemania I saw in the faces of the teenage girls in the audience, some so overwhelmed that they were literally crying. My sisters were screaming right along with them as we watched on TV. There we were, a part of it all, whether in the audience or one of the 73 million watching from their living rooms. That meant we were close to The Beatles. We were connected to the other fans and connected to the Fab Four themselves! And that allowed us to assign meaning to our lives.

We all want our lives to matter, to be significant. It is built into us. When I was a kid I memorized the song "Trouble" from the musical *The Music Man*. It was a long, talking song, and I memorized every word to perform for the *Muscular Dystrophy Labor Day Telethon* with Jerry Lewis. I was probably about seven years old. I remember we went to the telethon, and Donna Douglas, who played Elly May Clampett on the show *The Beverly Hillbillies*, was the guest presenter. Mom gave me some money to take up and give to the cause, and when I did Donna let me give her a kiss on the cheek, after which she let out one of her famous, ear-piercing whistles! I lived off that kiss for years. In fact, I still remember it. This famous star knew me, and I knew her. Heck, she had even let me kiss her! That kiss gave me a soul-satisfying sense of importance.

I'll never forget the day I met former President Bill Clinton. OK, it wasn't really him; it was an impersonator. But buddy, it felt like I really met him, and it made me feel really good. I had decided to join the ranks of presidential impersonators, and I was learning everywhere I could. I had seen Tim Watters, the world's number-one Bill Clinton impersonator, on TV many times, so I found him and asked him to lunch. Even though I knew this wasn't really the former president, I was so excited to meet him. It felt like I was going to meet the real president. When we shook hands I had a definite sense of exhilaration. I watched the people in the restaurant react to his presence, and I felt special personally. That's right, folks, that's me having lunch with the former president. Even though I clearly knew what was really going on, somehow my physicality couldn't tell the difference, and the rush of euphoria was a personal high I will always remember.

What the heck was that? Why was it so powerful? What is there to learn here?

As someone who is a dead ringer for George W. Bush (according to Dick Cheney, Barbara Walters, and lots of other really significant people—haha) I can and do have a similar impact on people wherever I go. I never think about how many people are watching me when I walk through the airport or the mall, but they watch. Every so often someone will just come up and ask for a picture. Sometimes they ask, "Are you really him?" I decided years ago to have fun with it, so sometimes I'll answer, "It's really me," which of course didn't answer the question they were really asking. They'll say, "I knew it!" At this point I'll spill the beans and use it to serve, inspire, and bless people.

I've watched people scream, wave, drop to their knees, and cry when I walked into a room because they think they are seeing their hero, my hero, George W. Bush. I know it's a grand illusion, an imitation—but it makes folks feel great, feel important, and even after I tell them I'm not really *Dubya*, the great feeling remains. I give people the feeling of being up close to true greatness, which helps them to feel important.

My joy is to give folks an encounter, an experience. But then I want to contrast that by making sure they know how awesome they are, how unique, how special. I want them to know that they're loved. Then, after their significance is established, I want them to forget about themselves and go and love somebody else, because true fulfillment comes from serving, loving, and giving. The echo of love is love!

Where does true significance come from?

My mom, Eileen Morgan, now residing in heaven, is not a famous person by any measurable standard, but to those who spoke at her life celebration (funeral) she couldn't have had a greater impact. Person after person came forward and told their story of how my mom's love and prayers had a huge impact on their life. Her strategy was simply to be obedient to her Savior, Jesus. She prayed for folks in churches, hospitals, and at her business. Because she loved her friends and even strangers deeply, she wanted the best for them, which meant she wanted Jesus for them. Her great, childlike faith was enough for her to pray about anything with folks, and amazing things happened on a regular basis. Her life was an adventure of friendship with the living, eternal King, and she was so fun to watch.

Lots of babies were born after she prayed for barren ladies. Our friends Rob and Lynette Swanson, for example, were unable to conceive for years. Doctors had told them Lynette would never be able to bear children because of scarring over more than 90 percent of her uterus. After Mom's healing prayer the chronic pain Lynette had felt in her body disappeared, and warmth flooded her belly. She conceived just a few weeks later, and they went on to have three wonderful children. The stories go on and on, and at our family business folks still come in and tell of the times my mom prayed for them and the impact those prayers had.

This is so significant because Mom had a dark start in life. Her poor parents put her into an orphanage when she was about five years old. The place was horrible, abusive, and uncaring. Eventually her parents retrieved her, but the fear of abandonment, of insignificance, followed her and hounded her. It influenced her decisions and informed her choices. She was able to overcome that fear with the knowledge that her wonderful Savior would never leave her, never abandon her. Out of that knowledge, deep in her heart, she wound up with a remarkable boldness in faith and loving people. Mom was able to overcome the feelings of insignificance thrust upon her during her childhood by embracing her identity as a child of God.

Any impact I ever have on this world is a direct result of Mom's significant influence on my life. When I was fifteen and fully invested in the sex, drugs, and rock 'n roll culture of our day, Mom gave her life to Jesus. She came alive with Christ and became so happy that the difference was impossible to ignore. I ran the other way for years, even while pretending I was a good little Christian boy. I was happy for mom, but I wasn't willing to give up my lifestyle. At age eighteen, on March 5, Mom dragged me to a church meeting, where I also became a Christian.

Following Mom's example, I am now committed to a life of true significance. I don't think Mom ever thought about her impact on the world or what kind of legacy she would leave. She was just dancing with her Savior, and every day was an adventure. I want to follow her lead, live by her example.

The Pebble in the Pond

When I speak I often talk about influence using the "pebble in a pond" illustration. When you drop the tiniest pebble into a pond, that pebble will break the surface of the water, causing small ripples of influence to be sent out in concentric, ever-expanding rings. There are two ways to increase this: more pebbles, or bigger rocks. It's all about impact.

When we were kids and we would go swimming, we would have contests to see who could make the biggest splash with our cannonball water entries. There was an art to entering the water with your body in just the right position to maximize your splash and drench the most people lounging alongside the pool.

When I speak to students I tell them, "Influence happens." If you speak loving words of encouragement, you are changing the world every day. If you speak harsh words that are mean and hateful, you are also changing the world.

> **If you speak loving words of encouragement, you are changing the world every day.**

The pebble represents you, and the act of dropping the pebble represents your words and actions. The water represents the people your influence impacts, and the ripples are the impact itself. There is a serious cause-and-effect that goes forth from you. Your words and deeds do not happen without influence. The first person they influence is you, because what you say, you will ultimately believe and become. We always move in the direction of our words. Henry Ford said, "Whether you think you can or you think you can't, you're right."

Years ago I got in the habit of concluding most conversations by saying the phrase, "God bless you." It's a nice parting salutation, and people almost always smile and say it back. It is, in fact, a prayer: "May God bless you," which is to say, "May God make you happy, or bring you happiness." I get blessed every time I say it. First, my ears hear me say it, and most of the time, the person I have just blessed will say something like, "Thank you. God bless you too." This is a great example of the ripple effect because I have had a positive influence on others, who have echoed back that prayer for blessing on my life.

Do you want to feel significant? Have a significant impact on others, even if it is just one pebble at a time. Again, at the risk of being redundant again, the echo of love is love!

I came from a loving home with a mom and a dad who cared for me. Still, at times I felt completely alone. I know this fear of not mattering is deep and powerful for many of us. The way I overcame my sense of worthlessness was to embrace a new identity in Jesus as a child of God. Then my new task was to take my eyes off myself, to change my focus, and to start trying to make a difference in the lives of others.

> *See what great love the Father has lavished*
> *on us, that we should be called children of*
> *God! And that is what we are!*
> —1 John 3:1, niv

With tenderness, God informs us that we are His own children, brothers and joint heirs of Jesus Himself. It's lofty to think about, but God's kids are His cherished sons and daughters. How's that for significant?

Genuine significance can be found in our identity with Christ and then in making a difference in a variety of ways. We love others, serve our communities, raise a family, and influence those around us. With all my heart I hope you will find your answer first in God and then in those who will love you just for who you are, and then use your powerful influence to make a difference in the lives of others. That's very significant.

My hope is to help as many people as I can to conquer the fear of insignificance by recognizing that every person has intrinsic, God-given worth. I want to encourage you to accept the love of your heavenly Father, whose specific love for you caused His Son to come to Earth to redeem mankind, with you in mind.

For God so loved [you]…that He gave His only begotten Son, that whoever believes in Him should not perish but have everlasting life.
—JOHN 3:16

So many people feel lost in the cosmos. You are not unseen. You are not abandoned. God knows you even if no one else does, and He loves you. He has already made the way for you to enjoy a very meaningful relationship with Him through His Son. You are welcome in His family.

CHAPTER 7

Fear of Man (or Woman)

Fear of man lays a snare, but whoever trusts in the LORD is safe.
—PROVERBS 29:25, ESV

*W*hat will they think of me? What will they do to me? What if I say something that offends someone? What if? What if? What if?

I am a fairly bold guy, but that wasn't always the case. I used to blend in with the wallpaper, trying to not draw attention to myself. "If they see me, it will be bad," I thought. I was a chameleon, without my own opinions or objections and without my own voice. I would say whatever I thought people wanted to hear. If life's a stage, I hid behind my curtain of fear and only popped out when I was sure nobody would hook me around the neck and yank me off the stage. After all the taunting and abuse I suffered as a kid, my final solution was just to shut up.

Perhaps you find yourself like most of us, allowing fear of what others think of you to have more influence over your life than you would like.

The young woman says, "I better sleep with him, or he won't love me anymore."

The father, stressed out over finances, obediently sends out an inflated invoice out of fear that his boss would fire him otherwise.

A single mom gives in to her teenage son. Why does she cave? Because she cowers in fear whenever he launches into a rage over not getting his way.

There are myriad young, unwed mothers, morally compromised men, frustrated moms, and delinquent teens destroyed by decisions made in the fear of man.

Decision-making is a process. Fear of man can influence every aspect of that process. This is huge. It's perhaps one of the greatest hindrances to our personal growth and professional advancement. How many times have you thought about or wanted to do something right and good—and trepidation about what others would say or think stopped you in your tracks?

As I have been writing this book, I must confess that the fear of man has been a continual nuisance to me. I keep wanting to apologize for the straight-up Christian content in the book because I don't want to offend those of you who may find it hard to relate to. But I keep plowing ahead because I'm writing from my heart. I'm sharing who I am and how I have dealt with various fears in my own life. Again, my goal here is to help you get over your fears. If I can't be authentic in the process I am giving in to fears myself.

One of the driving factors of my declaration of war on fear in the first place was my compassion for people who are dominated by the fear of man. I have a friend who is debilitated by the fear of offending someone. It creates rampant mis-under-indecisiveness and stress born out of a fear of making the wrong decisions. Do you sometimes feel like your feet are cemented to the floor because you're so afraid that your decisions will disappoint, anger, or hurt someone? You are not alone, but that fear is certainly not in your best interest.

Are you afraid to speak up or speak out or speak at all? Your opinions matter. Your voice is meant to be heard, for the good of yourself and those you care about. Your voice influences others. It has impact. It moves others. It can change their world!

> **Your voice influences others. It has impact. It moves others. It can change their world!**

Your fearful silence also speaks volumes. When you don't step up and share your thoughts when appropriate, your silence instructs others that you live in fear. Those who look up to you will surmise that living in fear is the thing to do. Imitation happens. It just does.

To move beyond fear you must recognize your God-given worth and the value of your contribution more than you fear any consequences coming from that contribution. The best thing for everyone is to speak the truth in a loving way. How people respond is not your responsibility. Being honest is. This is how we grow from fearful to courageous.

To expand on the pebble in the pond illustration from the previous chapter, if one lone voice is like a droplet of water on a glassy pond making a ripple that influences the rest of the water, then how much influence can two voices have? A dozen? A hundred? Think of the ripples on the water at the start of a spring rain. As the rain increases, the circles begin to intersect one another. The rain increases a little more, a little more. Now it is a thunderstorm. The influence of many people speaking with the same voice can change society—the world.

No wonder fear works overtime to keep us all silent! We have power over these phantom suggestions that hit our mind, causing us to act in a way that is less than who we are created to be, fearless.

Remember, too, that fear is also an emotion, and emotions are feelings, and feelings are fickle. They are not automatically based in truth. You can be personally hurt by something and then discover the thing never even happened, but you still feel hurt. My wife, Kathy, woke up feeling angry at our son Daniel because of something he did *in a dream!* As ridiculous as it sounds, it took a while before those feelings of anger began to dissipate.

Fearful thoughts attempt to make you "feel" afraid. The Bible character Nehemiah understood that. He was the king's cupbearer, who courageously faced the fear of man. He asked the king he was serving if he could have time off to go and help his people, the Israelites, rebuild their broken-down city. He led a group of ordinary citizens to rebuild the wall around Jerusalem. Once he started the massive project he was hit with a barrage of "fear-seeking missiles" when two of his enemies began mocking and taunting him, trying to use discouragement and fear to defeat the building project. They were attempting to stop the rebuilding project through the use of fear.

When Nehemiah's enemies did this, wise Nehemiah went directly to the Lord in prayer. He didn't engage with his enemies directly. He knew that to do so would only empower them and discourage his coworkers. He sought God's help and encouraged the builders to keep their focus on the task at hand.

These enemies didn't stop at taunting words. They went on to threaten violence against the builders to try to persuade them to abandon the project. Instead of quitting, Nehemiah encouraged them even further and outfitted them with weapons, underscoring the importance of the task. Even when an actual attack against them was planned, they kept building with a sword in one hand, a trowel in the other. Eventually, due to the courage and commitment of the builders, and Nehemiah's wise leadership, the project was completed.

> ## Fear gains power as we contemplate it.

Fear gains power as we contemplate it. If Nehemiah had stopped and pondered the threats and taunts of his enemies, those threats would have gained power over him. In our lives, we have the choice to act with courage or to stop and ponder the fearful thoughts that try to hold us back. We can protect our own minds from allowing fear to gain a foothold in our lives.

> *I have stored up your word in my heart, that I might not sin against you.*
> —PSALM 119:11, ESV

I have found that as I ignore my fears and act in the way courage dictates, fear dissipates like smoke moving out of the way of a solid object. I saw an illustration of this recently during a night out at the movies. In a tense scene from the adventure movie *Jurassic World*, a deadly velociraptor is chasing the stars of the film. When he sees the projected holographic image of another dinosaur, he stops temporarily to attack the image. As soon as he figures out it's not real, he passes right through it like it's nothing. That's what we can do with fear. We can let the smokescreen stop us, or we can courageously pass right through it.

If we stay on the fear side of our smokescreens and dinosaurs and people, the feelings of fear and fear's influence become stronger. If God says, "Do not be afraid," then to ponder fear is more than an idle pastime; it's the road to ruin. There is a word to define a mental image of terror or dread. It is the word *spectre*. Fear is a "spectre projector," showing you scenes of a phantom menace or huge dinosaur or mother-in-law in your path.

We deal with things like the fear of being fired, our spouse leaving us, our kids messing up, a lack of finances, etc. There may be an element of truth in the risk of something bad happening, but fear is not fair. It amplifies the negative and blocks any image of a positive outcome. Fearful images may be big and even seem real on the spectre projector, but they are just an illusion.

OK, it's time to talk about the elephant in the room. To train an elephant, trainers will chain them to a post when they're small. Eventually the elephant gives up tugging on the chain, knowing they can't get free. Once the elephant gives up the hope of being free, trainers can take the chain away, and the elephant won't leave because the chain still exists in his mind. Elephants never forget. We can be like that, never forgetting the past hurt or pain that keeps us afraid, or, with God's help, we can walk away from the phantom chain into the tender arms of Jesus. Remember, fear is a phantom. It may seem big, but it's just an *elephantom. Ba dum, tss!*

We have all had the pain of people letting us down, rejecting us, criticizing us, abandoning us, being angry at us, disappointing us, or discouraging us. These are very real experiences that etch our memory. The pain is real. But fear takes past hurts and amplifies them, attaches them to our current circumstances, and projects them into our future. They appear as huge barriers to us moving forward. Fear makes the projected phantom pain of the future even greater than the pain of the past. Have you ever said, "I'll never let that happen again," or, "I won't go through that again" or, "I won't let myself be vulnerable again" or, "I will never risk, trust, love, care, or try again." or, "I'll probably disappoint, anger, or let people down."?

We act on what we actually believe. If we believe that these fear-of-man-based projections will come to pass, we will shrink back from everything in life we were created to do and be. We'll be afraid to take risks, act courageously, love people, lead people, or serve people.

Part of the fear of man is fear of the unknown. But once you have taken fear on and overcome it, it gets easier and easier to do it the second time, the third time, until fear eventually has no hold over you, as you grow to live a courageous lifestyle.

A good lifelong friend of ours, Bob, grew up without a father, but the kindest thing he ever heard his male authority figure say to him was, "You should have been twins, because no one person should be that stupid." Yet Bob pushed past the fear of rejection. Rather than wallow in the fear of being hurt again he uses his life to help others who have been hurt. He spends his life "loving the least of these." He now serves by leading conferences and has had a huge impact on many lives, including mine.

One way I battle fear is to have a posture of being ready to serve at a moment's notice. If I see someone or even a group of people who look despondent or downhearted, I try to immediately obey those nudges to reach out. Those nudges can come to me in taxicabs, grocery store lines, or even in airports. One day I was standing in line about to board a flight when a thought hit my mind out of nowhere. *"Sing to everybody."* Huh? I felt distinctly like the Lord was instructing me just to turn around and belt out a song to everybody waiting to board this flight. My first thought was, "Oh no!" Then I thought, "That's just me trying to draw attention to myself." After I thought about it I realized, "No, I don't even want to do this, and I'm not the least bit interested in drawing attention to myself. In fact, I'm really nervous that this might actually be the Lord directing me."

I silently turned inward to prayer and said, "Lord, if there is any way, please take this cup (song) from me, but not my will but Yours." I felt a confirmation in my heart to sing, so I looked to my left wondering how this was going to play out and saw a guy who I thought was the captain of the flight. I just said to him kinda loudly, "Hey, captain, I'm proud to be an American," and led right into the chorus of Lee Greenwood's 'God Bless the USA." Then I turned to the rest of the two hundred or so people waiting to board the flight and finished the chorus, inviting them to join along and sing. I'm not sure if anybody sang with me that day, but one thing I do know: my song definitely lightened the mood of everybody getting on the flight. Everyone was more talkative to his or her neighbors, and there was just generally a friendlier atmosphere for the rest of the flight.

A guy came up to me after the flight and struck up a conversation. After a bit I shared with him what I do, and he told me he leads conferences. He expressed an interest in having me come speak at one of his events. We don't always see the immediate effects of immediate obedience, but we can be confident that as we courageously obey it releases God's work in our lives and the lives we influence.

Divine Appointment

One day I spoke at a motivational event in Chicago. During the daylong event I was standing in the lobby of the convention center talking to a friend when a couple walked up to me to get a "photo with the President." As they were approaching, the word *eternity* flashed across my mind, and I felt nudged to share my own faith story with them. I began by asking them if they ever ponder the mysteries of eternity. I said, "Isn't it fantastic to think about?" The young lady lit up like it was really important to her, and I proceeded to share with them how they could know where they would spend their forever. I shared my own, personal faith testimony, ending with telling them that I was born again on March 5th, 1975. She lit up again, gasped, and exclaimed, "That's the very day I was born."

And so this became the very day she and her friend were born again, as I was privileged to introduce them to the Savior. I could so easily have ignored that subtle little word picture, *eternity*, and just taken a photo with these folks and been done with it. How often we either ignore those gentle nudges or shrink back in fear, refusing to obey the promptings. But what do we lose when fear wins? What opportunities are missed? What lives are never transformed? What relationships are never reconciled?

God's divine appointments await those who don't shrink back in fear. These are the kinds of adventures God is pleased to share with those that trust Him and push past the fear of man. These are His intentions for us and His invitations to join Him in glorious adventure! Don't miss out!

> # God's divine appointments await those who don't shrink back in fear.

Maybe that's why God is not pleased with us when we shrink back. He knows how devastating it is when we miss divine opportunities and how glorious it is when we partner with Him to see lives transformed. His motivation is not anger when we fail; it is love.

> *But My righteous one [the one justified by faith] shall live by faith...And if he draws back [shrinking in fear], My soul has no delight in him.*
> —HEBREWS 10:38, AMP

God knows that through our obedience to Him we and those we influence can receive all that He has for us—unbroken peace, complete provision, joy unspeakable, a full, abundant life, and even some hidden treasures.

One day as a young, single Christian I was in Ormond Beach in the lobby of a hotel about to check in to begin a wonderful weekend of swimming, volleyball, and frivolity with friends. There in the lobby I saw a handicapped fellow I recognized from Orlando. I sensed God directing me to reach out to him. I didn't want to do it, but I obeyed

God rather than my fear of reaching out, and Dave and I began a friendship. The next night, Dave introduced me to my wife—*to my wife!* Now, this true story deserves its own book, which one day I expect I'll write. But imagine what our glorious God might want to give to you through the simple act of obedience. Do you see what a costly poison fear is? Friend, don't give the enemy one more victory over your life. Choose to trust God rather than the lies of fear! What could be more important?

The next time you get a simple nudging to help someone, to speak to someone, to call or text someone, go for it! You will be blown away by the great way God wants to use you during the course of everyday life. Next time you are reading the Bible and a scripture seems to come alive, don't ignore it. Stop and pray, then listen to see if God is revealing something to you or about you, or prompting you to some action.

So what's the answer to the question, What will they think of me? To me the more relevant question is, What will God think of me? In other words, I have a genuine love for Jesus that makes me want to please Him. I want to do His will and glorify Him with my life. This love is a big motivator of my obedience. John 15 says, "If you love Me you will do what I command, and My command is this: love one another" (author's paraphrase). This loving command informs my decision to take the risk of obedience. You can't love people and shrink back in fear at the same time.

What is the real risk anyway? Is it actually riskier to obey God or the one who we know is lying to keep us from obeying God? Who is our friend, and who is our enemy? Obeying God is presented to our minds as fear and risk only by the one who wants us to distrust God. So I say it's time to raise up an army of brave, obedient sons and daughters who love God and look like God and act like God.

Be imitators of God, as beloved children.
And walk in love, as Christ loved us and gave

himself up for us, a fragrant offering and sacrifice to God.

—EPHESIANS 5:1–2, ESV

Joel, who is writing this book with me, had a dream last night. He didn't know what I was about to write when I said, "We can be like God and look like God and act like God." As soon as I wrote that (we are FaceTiming and sharing a Google doc, so we are both working together in real time) Joel informed me of his dream, in which people were coming up to him asking him if he was God! He was asking others if they were God. Joel said that in the dream asking this question stirred a spiritual awakening in people. The point is that we are truly called to be partakers of the divine nature. God lives in us, and we are called to be His image-bearers.

Be true to the image of God in you. We are called to look like our Father, to act like our Father, and to be like our Father, for truly He is in us and with us.

I am a George W. Bush impersonator. I am clearly not George W. Bush, but when I do my best work, people think I am. I've met George W. Bush a few times, but we haven't spent any significant time together, and we don't talk on a regular basis. Yet, I look like him, sound like him, and represent (re-present) him to people who say I am a spitting image of him. It's kinda cool how much I respect him and want to emulate him.

Yet, George W. Bush does not live in me. But God does live in me, and we communicate with one another all day long. We are called by our Father to be like Him, to represent Him so the world can know Him, and to live the coolest, most excellent life of obedience ever.

The difference is that God does live in us. When we imitate Him, that imitation is empowered by His actual presence in our lives. It's God living in us and through us.

Jesus said, "I am the light of the world," in John 8:12, but His declaration didn't end there. He turned around and said to His disciples, "*You* are the light of the world" (Matt. 5:14, emphasis added). Is it the same light? Is it a counterfeit light? It *is* the very same light—the light of God and the lamp of truth. We represent God, who truly lives in us and desires to live through us.

We were created in God's image to represent Him to people. Like a blanket, fear covers over the image of God in us. If we hide under the cover of fear, we hide ourselves from the very things we were created to do and be. God understands that we have a tendency to be fearful people, so He clothes us with courage and gifts us with grace to come out from under the cover of fear. Then we can boldly face the interactions we encounter every day and obey the call to love others.

> # Like a blanket, fear covers over the image of God in us.

At its root fear's real goal is to pull us away from God, from trusting Him and walking by faith. If we develop our faith and trust in God and our obedience to Him, over time, step by glorious step, we will grow in our faith and relegate fear to a distant nuisance.

Fear of negative reactions from other people, an inordinate need to be loved and accepted, the desire to maintain the status quo and not make waves—these are all based in a desire to gain security from people. These fears of man constantly attempt to pull us from a place of trust and joy. But real security doesn't come from people; it only comes from our relationship with God.

When I was younger I had a really, really hard time voicing an opinion. I didn't want to be in disagreement with folks because I didn't want to face their disapproval. This was huge in me as a teen. To be honest, it is something that I still struggle with.

I think a lot of fear of man is generational. I come from a family of ostriches. Traditionally, we are very comfortable with our head in the sand. Confrontation is just not our thing. Saying the thing that needs to be said provokes all kinds of trepidation in my family.

Some folks fear confrontation in families, and some fear it in business also. Fear of confrontation can lead to mutiny, a vacuum of leadership, and chaos in the workplace. Being willing to confront a situation, when handled with grace and appropriate humility, can be heroic and so important.

To be a leader, to have influence in the lives of others, you have to be willing to say what needs to be said, even at the risk of sometimes being misunderstood. You have to be willing to say things that may not be popular or appreciated.

If speaking out on a subject is the right thing in a given circumstance, but we don't speak out because of fear, then we've done the wrong thing by remaining silent. Why is that OK with us? I still at times will allow fear to beat me. But I don't want that ever to be the case. I don't want to cower in fear when I should be saying and doing what's right. I am not OK with just saying, "Oh, well. This is just me. Don't judge me."

One thing that has helped me and so many others to be successful in doing the right thing in the face of fear or opposition is being well prepared in advance. Fear can't easily get a foothold in someone with regard to an activity they have done over and over, practiced beforehand, or decided ahead of time.

The headlines all read something like this: "New York Giants wide receiver Odell Beckham Jr. makes the greatest catch of 2014 and arguably of all time." With a defender hanging on him and committing blatant pass interference, Odell Beckham Jr. jumped up and reached out with one hand to snag a speeding football thrown fifty-two yards. He caught the ball behind his head with one hand at the front corner of the end zone. The announcers said, "How in the world? He is insane. How do you make that catch? That is impossible!" It seemed like a miracle. People said it was an amazing fluke, but a pregame video told a different story.

The pregame video was of Beckham practicing catching the ball with one hand over and over again. From watching the video it was clear that Beckham had made this catch hundreds, if not thousands, of times before. So when it came time for the big game and that pass was thrown, it wasn't a miracle; it was muscle memory.[1]

We need brain memory and faith memory when it comes to the big games and big challenges of our lives. It is these moments of decision, these defining moments we need to be prepared for. The outcome of these situations may be shocking to others, but they will be no surprise to us and God, for we will have been well prepared in advance.

If you must take a stand in a sudden moment and preparation is not possible, doing the right thing is something you can prepare your heart for. If you condition yourself, your heart and mind, determining that you are going to be a person of character and courage, you are far more likely to opt for the courageous action when the need arises.

I used to be pretty cowardly, and I had never imagined myself taking a bold stand. I would choose not to participate in conversations for fear of alienating one side or the other. Now I can picture myself taking a stand and being willing to step up when a situation calls for it, and I have spent time praying for God's help to be courageous.

You might be a dad who wants to start a Bible study in your home, but you are afraid you kids will think you're kooky.

You might be a student who has a conviction to take a stand against bullying and to defend someone who needs a friend, but you fear losing your cool friends.

Perhaps you're a mom being invited by other moms to a bar, but you know they are flirting with disaster. You know you shouldn't go, but you just got accepted by the group.

The Bush family motto is "Do the right thing."[2] The best time to choose to do the right thing is before the choice presents itself. When we face challenging decisions, the longer we wait to decide, the stronger the voice of fear grows. Deciding beforehand to automatically do the right thing is a strong defense that renders fear powerless.

Just writing this book has been a huge exercise in overcoming the fear of man. Any time you voice an opinion you open yourself up to criticism. But if I'm called to do that—and I believe I am—to shrink back is cowardly. I've been there; I know. But I am determined to move past the fear of man to speak the truth and speak it in love.

My cowboy hat's off to you for running past the smoke screens and false projections of fear. I can see you walking boldly into the clear air of victory over the fears that once held sway over you! You are a champion, not in your own strength but empowered by the One who called you to live full and boldly as a child of the King!

PHOTOS

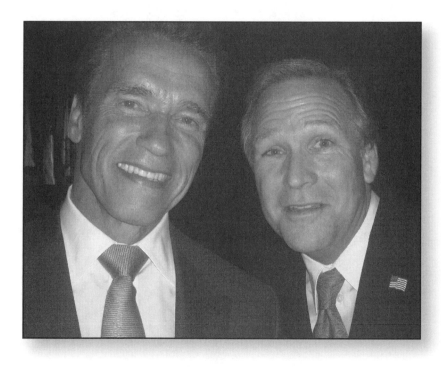

At Arnold's birthday party. Hey Arnold,
we should do a movie together!

The great motivator Brian Tracy
taught me to "Eat that Frog."

Before performing at The Comedy and
Magic Club in Hermosa Beach, CA.

Comedic Roots? My mom and dad
kept us all laughing growing up.

Chewing the fat with Franklin Graham,
son of Billy Graham

The very moment we found out
Kathy is healed of Hepatitis C!

Backstage with James Robison and Gov. Mike Huckabee.
Name dropping? Me? Never!

For the best in Free World Leadership,
ya just can't beat the Bushes!

Star Spangled Couple. Kathy and I
as Laura and George.

Me in prosthetic mask as John McCain

Fun with Mirrors

Pastor Joel Osteen

Getting to know Phil Robertson of Duck Dynasty.
Talk about Fearless!

I was privileged to tour with Sean Hannity.
Sarah Palin is actually my friend Patsy Gilbert.

Finally met my hero! He famously said,
"If I had a face like mine, I'd be mad as hell!"

CHAPTER 8

Fear of Public Speaking

Everyone who has ever opened his or her mouth and uttered words to communicate to another person is already a public speaker. We're all already public speakers. We speak in public, unafraid. The only difference is the size of the audience.

By public speaking, we are talking about communication and influence. People interacting with people. Overcoming this fear will open wide so many possibilities for your influence and impact. Let's see if we can make this unknown, known. Shedding some light on public speaking in general will make it a bit more familiar and a lot less scary. We can all agree influence happens, and that influence begins with relationships.

Understanding this concept will allow us to scale this monster to a manageable problem. Each small victory leads to a bigger win as the challenges and triumphs grow step by step. A student breaks through the wall of fear to talk to another student at their lockers. Once that fear is conquered, he has the confidence to feel comfortable contributing to a discussion in a small, casual group in class. This victory leads to the next hurdle: the fear of giving speeches in class. And it continues. Over time and with a commitment to overcoming fear, that student realizes that speaking to an audience of twenty peers is not any scarier than engaging one of them at a time. It is just a matter of expanding influence.

At whatever stage of life you find yourself now, you take part in relationships that make up your circle of influence. As you push the limits of your relational comfort zone, engaging in conversations with "audiences" of various sizes, you'll find that the walls of fear surrounding that type of public speaking will fall, and your circle of influence will expand. You see, we were born to give and receive love. We were created with a need to be a part of other people's lives. It's just so much better if we're intentional about it.

> You see, we were born to give and receive love. We were created with a need to be a part of other people's lives.

Some people break out in a cold sweat when you even mention getting in front of a group, let alone on a stage to speak. For some the fear of public speaking is greater even than the fear of dying. Some folks get visibly shaken. Their hearts start beating faster and their palms start sweating when they just think about how they would feel getting on stage in front of an audience of say, ten thousand people—or even at a meeting of ten.

Frankly, I'm not one of those people. I honestly have little fear of public speaking. I love it. I thrive on it. I run to the microphone. For the many times I have gotten in front of live audiences in say, China or Japan or Germany or in a World Cup Soccer Stadium, I can honestly say that fear of public speaking doesn't really scare me, except at the Comedy and Magic Club near Los Angeles, California.

Until then I'd never performed a set at a comedy club. Those audiences will eat you alive. I have been asked why I never joined the comedy club circuit. Why not take the route most comedians take? Fear. Fear of rejection. Fear of the unknown. Fear of forgetting my lines and peeing my pants while being hit by a flying shoe.

But I was there, facing my fear, slaying this dragon at the famous Comedy and Magic Club in Hermosa Beach, a suburb of Los Angeles![1] This is the same club where on any given Sunday you're likely to find one of Jay Leno's amazing cars parked out front. Lining the back stage walls are signed photos of the comedy greats who have performed on that stage. In the green room the cinder block walls have been hand-decorated with signatures and artwork by legendary comedians throughout the years. And here I am looking at the door where legend after legend walked through, and my name is on the lineup sheet.

I was on in about three minutes. I felt my pulse quickening, so I went and stood behind the curtain, listening to the very funny host of the evening doing her set. Right on the other side of this curtain was my future. This performance was being recorded to make a promo video for some of the most influential people in the comedy and entertainment world. I tried not to picture the audience as a bunch of hungry sharks, but I felt the fear approaching. I thought, "Wait a minute, I'm writing a book on fear. I can't let fear do this to me!" So I prayerfully resisted the fear, and as I did, something wonderful happened.

I heard God speak to my heart, saying, "You know I'm a present help in time of need. Why don't you ask Me for my perspective?"

I prayed, "Oh, yeah. God, You're alive and well, and You communicate. OK, Lord, what do you want me to know right now at this very moment as I'm about to step out onto that stage?"

I heard God tell me three distinct things. First, that of all the places in the world I could be, I was in the exact right place at the exact right time. I could feel fear leaving. Second, God reminded me that He who loves me most is in me. This was such a comfort, as He elaborated: "I, who, died on the cross for you, who truly loves you most, am right here with you and in you. You will not be on that stage alone." It was a tender moment. Oh, how "perfect love casts out fear" (1 John 4:18).

What He said next was all I needed. God said, "I know and love each and every person in that audience, and I want to love them through you." That was it. It was the swivel that changed the whole focus of my thoughts. "Oh, yeah," I reminded myself, "it's not about me." I was ready to go out there and be a vessel of God's love to that audience. And from what I could perceive, that's what happened. Now, I didn't mention God or religion or anything like that. I just did my best to connect through comedy.

My focus became one of God's love for the audience, each and every person. As the curtain opened, instead of fearful thoughts I was gifted with a sense of love for each one I saw. As I began my scripted routine I wasn't just reciting memorized lines; I was communicating love and joy to individuals. I felt a sense of connection with those folks that translated into a wonderful rapport and peals of laughter.

Fear of public speaking is a form of performance anxiety. It has to do with the fear of disapproval and the fear of rejection—fear of shoes, eggs, and rotten tomatoes being thrown in your direction. People get short of breath at the mere thought of getting up in front of all those probing eyes. We tend to "pre-magine'"what the event will be like, and fear projects the worst that could happen into our imagination. (Remember the spectre projector.) This leads to an escalation of the sweaty-palmed anxiety we were already feeling. I've often heard the advice to picture your audience in their underwear to overcome nervousness. I don't recommend it. Tried it once. Scary.

When you're a teenager the approval of your peers is of greatest concern. I'll never forget the time I froze in front of six hundred of them.

I had heard the song "The Christmas Guest," performed by Johnny Cash and written by Helen Steiner Rice. It was a moving poem put to music. It just so happened that our youth group Christmas party was several weeks away, so I called my youth pastor and asked him if he would like me to perform the song for the Christmas party. He called me back only a few days before the party and asked me if I could still do it. In my enthusiasm I said yes. Mind you, I had not even begun memorizing the poem and did not have a copy of it on hand.

"What did I just do?" I asked myself as panic threatened to grip my heart. But I knew I could do this! I started feeling the pressure big time. I got my Craig portable cassette tape recorder ready and called the local country music station and asked them to play the song. I told them that I needed to memorize it and that I was really crushed for time. I was pleased when they played the song within about an hour of my request, and I hit record as I held my cassette recorder in front of my family console stereo. I recorded the song and started playing it over and over again, memorizing line after line. With each passing hour I felt the mixture of the joy in the opportunity and the pressure to get it right. I got to where I could say the whole poem without stopping, even adding some strumming chords on my acoustic guitar.

The night of the party came, and I was ready. I was excited because I had said the poem so many times without messing up. The time came for our youth pastor to introduce me. I took the stage, feeling ready. I began the poem flawlessly, comfortably, and after about the second line I just forgot everything.

A cold sweat broke out on my red-hot face. I just stared at the crowd. I thought they would boo me off the stage, but they didn't. They were staring back as though urging me on, trying to pull the words out of my throat. They were for me, not against me. Not what I would have expected. At least that was comforting. Our youth pastor, Alex, jumped up on the stage and put his arm around my shoulder and comfortingly recalled his first time in front of an audience when he was younger. Just taking the eyes of the room off of me for ten seconds gave me enough of a release from the fear that the next line of the poem came to me. Thankfully, I was able to pick up where I left off and finished the performance to a gracious ovation.

I'm so grateful for the encouraging feedback I received. Had I gotten laughter, jeers, and rotten tomatoes, you might not be reading these words now. It helps to know that in most speaking situations people really are for you. They want you to do well.

If people are for you, how much more is God for you!

> # If people are for you, how much more is God for you!

Right before a performance, speech, television appearance, or interview, I pray. For me this is an important part of my preparation. It serves several purposes for me. Prayer reminds me of my dependence upon God in every endeavor but mostly the one upon which I am about to embark. I want not only to position myself for God's help but to be quick to acknowledge and thank Him for that help when it arrives, as it always does.

God is faithful, and I am trying to be. I ask Him to help me be successful not merely for my benefit but for the benefit of the folks who've invested their time to be there. I am aware that time is a precious, limited commodity, more valuable than money, because each moment is its own micro universe, in itself utterly irreplaceable. If someone or a group of people have invested their moments for no other purpose than to listen to and learn from me, I count that as precious and priceless, and I do not want to squander their limited time by not doing my best. That's why I pray!

I want to be grateful to my Creator for helping me to complete each successful presentation, and frankly, sometimes I get caught up with folks at the end of a performance taking pictures and kissing babies. So, I tell Him thank you up front and honor Him as the One who gave me life, breath, and comedic timing.

Also, I pray as a witness. When I have a group of volunteer youngsters playing the role of the pretend Secret Service agents for one of my George W. Bush performances, I ask them to pray with me for all the above reasons and because it's good to see folks outwardly and fearlessly dependent upon God. Lead by example.

Prayer works! Another reason I pray is simply that—who knew?— God answers prayer. Studies have been done on the statistical number of people who recover from illness when prayer is involved. Scientists will praise prayer as some sort of psychological healing elixir while denying the obvious. There is a God to whom those prayers ascend who takes pleasure in meeting the needs of His people. Prayer does indeed work, because God answers prayer. Any loving father listens to the requests of his beloved children and will give them what they ask if they ask for something that is good for them.

> *If a son asks for bread from any father among you, will he give him a stone? Or if he asks for a fish, will he give him a serpent instead of a fish?*
>
> —LUKE 11:11

We are implored by our heavenly Dad not only to ask, seek, and knock but to do so persistently, repeatedly, as a force of habit. I believe that my consistent habit of prayer is one of the main reasons I have obtained a measure of success.

Prayer is foundational in overcoming the fear of public speaking. But we must build with preparation. It has been said that proper preparation prevents poor performance. When I first asked for permission to recite the poem at my youth group I should have begun learning the piece just in case. There is no substitute for preparation.

Nothing opens the door to cold-blooded panic like not knowing what you're going to say when you step up to a microphone in front of a group of people.

On the other hand, knowing your topic like the back of your hand and being well prepared puts you in the driver's seat! It makes you the authority, and it earns you the ear of your listeners. Panic turns to peace as you take your listeners down roads you've driven on many, many times.

This point was driven home to me when I got cheered like a champion but then booed off the stage in front of a national audience on prime time TV. That day I went from what seemed like the highest of highs to the lowest of lows in about sixty seconds.

It was my prime time, go-for-the-gold moment on a major reality TV show competition in front of a live audience in Dallas, Texas! It was right where George W. Bush himself is their bigger-than-life hometown hero! Everybody thought I would rock it, including me. I should have been spending weeks of uninterrupted time working out every word, pouring over reruns of the show, visualizing the pathway to my success. I even had help from a previous champion of the show who now has a thriving show of his own. He and I had become acquaintances in Los Angeles when I was on another reality show and in the top ten. He advised me with respect to how to pass the audition. His advice: "Bring your *A game*! If you don't get past the audition it won't matter what you had in your back pocket."

It's not that I didn't prepare, but I didn't prepare wisely and I didn't take my acquaintance's wise advice. I felt that I needed to hold back my best bit for later in the show, assuming that I would pass the audition. I argued this to him, and his comeback now rings like a prophecy.

I thought it would be a slam-dunk because of the natural gift that God has put in me to look and act so much like George W. Bush. How I wish I had read John Maxwell's book *Talent Is Never Enough*. Talent will get you to the plate, but only preparation and practice will train you to knock the ball out of the park!

> **Talent will get you to the plate, but only preparation and practice will train you to knock the ball out of the park!**

Here's what happened. As I walked out onto that stage in Dallas to the strains of "Hail to the Chief," everyone sprang to their feet and started cheering and clapping loudly. Cheering is an understatement. They were shouting. They were ecstatic. The well-known celebrity judges kept looking around at the crowd, who just got louder and louder in their praise for their hometown hero, their national champion, George W. Bush. I'll never know how many people in the audience thought it was actually the president stopping by for a greeting and how many were simply loaning this entertainer their love for Dubya. But either way, the cheers were absolutely thunderous! It was all good—until I opened my mouth. That's where my lack of preparation sabotaged my performance.

I failed to recognize the amazing thing that was going on in that moment and the genuine love being poured toward the stage by that audience of Dallas residents. Instead of authentically engaging with those folks or conversing with the judges, like I would have if I'd watched the show enough, I began with canned, cheesy remarks that had nothing to do with what was happening. Slowly those shouts and cheers turned into jeers and boos. As enthusiastically as I was welcomed, I was rejected! *Buzz, buzz, buzz.* I can still hear Sharon Osbourne's comments echo in my soul: "Well, you certainly look like him, but your material isn't strong." *Ouch!*

That day I learned one of life's biggest lessons: Don't expect a great presentation without proper preparation. Remember Odell Beckham Jr. from the last chapter?

There are three keys to preparation: practice, practice, practice.

Sit down and negotiate with yourself to find the resolve to

practice until you are very comfortable with your material and delivery. It's easy to think that great speakers are just naturally gifted, and though there is some truth to that, every effective presenter must still practice. Preparation alleviates so much of the fear of speaking, because the speech and the performance have been lived by you over and over before you actually get there. It is just a fact that if you know your material better than anyone else in the room it will make you more confident, and it will give everyone else confidence in you. Folks will trust you to speak into their lives if you know what you're talking about.

Practicing your talk until you really know it will make you comfortable with the material. Practice in front of your mirror, your spouse, or nonjudgmental friends who understand what you are doing. This will also help you feel comfortable when it really counts, because you will have been there before. It won't seem like you are without a compass in unknown territory. You'll have much less to fear.

It may also be helpful for you to attend some workshops on public speaking. There's a really great resource available to train you on stage presence, how to connect with your audience, and how to prepare a great speech. It was created by my dear friend, communicator Ken Davis. It's called *Dynamic Communicators*. There is a link to his website on www.WarOnFearBook.com. I have attended this conference several times and greatly benefited from this fun and foundational workshop. If you are a communicator, you've got to check it out! Much of what I've learned about public speaking came from Ken's teaching.

Remember, be yourself! Everyone else is already trying to be somebody else. People think they have to be like someone else or be something else in order to be a good speaker, but there's really no substitute for being authentic. Experts tell us the number one indicator of effective speaking is putting you and your listeners at ease and being yourself. Create empathy by being vulnerable. When you are authentic and share some ways that you have done it wrong, blown it, or flat-out failed, your audience will feel more connected to you, more trusting. If you can do it with humor, all the better.

> Experts tell us the number one indicator of effective speaking is putting you and your listeners at ease and being yourself.

If you have the option, speak on material you feel passionate about. That will help you to be yourself. While we admire the speeches of our favorite orators, it's better if you don't try to be someone you're not. Unless you are playing the role of a character, being yourself will relieve you of the fear and pressure of performance or acting, and you can just relax and try to enjoy the time together speaking to friends.

Finally, while being genuinely yourself, your focus should be on your listeners and their benefit. Think about your content. Stay passionate about the message. That's what's important. People want you to succeed; they're almost always pulling for you. When you present in a prepared, authentic, caring way, it makes them feel good about themselves and their decision to listen to you.

If you are approaching the podium for the first time, you will probably experience some apprehension no matter how well prepared you are. But, well prepared you will be, and because you've practiced, muscle memory will kick in. You'll do fine. With repeated opportunities, you'll be more familiar and less afraid.

Nothing can warp you past your first speaking experience, but once you've done it, you've done it.

There. That wasn't so bad was it? Take it all in stride. With practice, you'll get better, guaranteed. I can't guarantee that you'll never wet your pants on stage, but if you're worried about it, come prepared. Adult diapers come in many sizes.

If you will do the hard work of preparation, commit to being authentic, and overcome the temptation to make it all about you, you can overcome the fear of public speaking. Go get 'em, tiger!

Happy speaking!

CHAPTER 9

Fear of Missing Out

FOMO No Mo!

If you don't read this chapter *right now* you'll miss out on life-changing truths and forever pay the price! Plus, if you do read it right now, you alone will have special access to a never-to-be-repeated special offer! So don't miss out. But wait! There's more...

The fear of missing out (FOMO) whispers to your brain, "Somewhere, someone is having more fun than me." It also shouts, "If you decide to help your friend move, you'll miss the movie your other friends are going to."

We walk confidently into the grocery store with a short list. A few minutes later we're standing in the middle of the cereal aisle paralyzed thinking to ourselves, "If I get the fruity, nutty flaky clusters I'll miss the roasted granola honey crunches." Starbucks or Dunkin Donuts? Home Depot or Lowe's? Craigslist or eBay? *Ahhh! I can't choose!*

There are two sides to the FOMO coin. One keeps you incessantly moving, trying to do everything lest you miss out on something. The other paralyses you, keeping you from choosing anything because you are afraid you'll make the wrong choice. Either way, you are being led around by fear.

Fear of missing out traps us in frantic activity as we succumb to the tyranny of the urgent. Jerry Seinfeld talks about racehorses. He says that they run with all their might, just to end up where they started. He suggests that they should just stay where they are, and they would be the first one to the finish line. We can avoid a lot of running around in circles (or ovals), getting nowhere, if we resist the fear of missing out. Plus, Seinfeld also says, "They never tell the horses that if they run so fast they trip and break a leg, they get shot!"[1] When we run around FOMOing at the mouth, the enemy never tells us he is trying to trip us up.

FOMO can also keep us from running the race altogether. If we're afraid to make a choice, we'll get nowhere, tormented by fears like, "What if I'm in the wrong race or getting off track?" Second guesses, second thoughts, distraction, and reconsideration are what this type of FOMO is all about.

When we make a choice, it eliminates all other choices. We fear that one of those other choices may be better than what we have already chosen or another alternative, so we don't choose. Or we choose one thing and then the other over and over again. To open the door to Alaska is to close the door to Hawaii and every place else. As long as we don't decide anything at all every choice remains available, until time runs out and no choice at all is left. Soon the night is over, all the planes have flown, and you're lonely and alone in the airport standing in the last remaining open store unable to choose between the Snickers and the KitKat bar.

Failure to commit is rampant because people fear that if they commit to one person, one invitation, or one activity someone or something better will come along, and they will miss out. Even when people commit there seems to be an epidemic of lack of keeping commitments when something "better" comes along. Litanies of excuses replace keeping our word. It seems we are always looking over our shoulder or at our phone screens for someone that is doing something better than what we're doing right now.

Teens and adults have conversations and meetings while constantly checking their texts, tweets, and Facebook messages. Moms try to give their kids attention while checking posts about all the fun their single friends are having at concerts, cruises, and ski slopes. Then they think, "Why did I marry this slob?" while the single woman on the ski slopes hopes she'll meet a man to marry.

Fear of missing out churns out regret.

How many gym memberships have we signed up for during a special offer but rarely used? Yet we're still paying because we don't wanna miss out on using it someday, usually January 2 through 5. How many two-hour Facebook sessions have kept us from the sleep we need, even though we can't remember one thing someone posted? How many texts while driving have caused accidents? How many FOMO distractions have cheapened or ruined real relationships? "I know I promised to spend the day with you, honey, but Greg wants to go play golf." The fear of missing out is costly.

> ## The fear of missing out is costly.

Literally while we were writing this, Joel got a prerecorded phone message. He said he just had to check it in case it was something important. (He says he is a work in progress.) The voice said, "This is a call about your credit card. There are no problems with your account right now, but this is the final notice for you to receive an interest rate as low as 1 percent. This is your final notice. So that you don't miss out on this limited time offer, press 'one' on your phone now." Like most of us, he was tempted to press "one" lest he miss out on this too-good-to-pass-up offer.

This scam plays on our fear of missing out and has led thousands of people to give out personal information that scammers use to steal money and destroy the credit of unsuspecting people. Does that sound familiar?

> *The thief comes only to steal and kill and destroy; I have come that they may have life, and have it to the full.*
> —John 10:10, NIV

Beer commercials seem to promise that if you come down to the bar you'll find the fun and camaraderie you've always wanted. Car ads are created so the prospective customer will see himself in the driver's seat, peeling out, sliding into the front of that club where the astonishingly beautiful girl gives him that sensuous glance of approval. The not-so-subtle message is drawing him magnetically to the dealership, because if you don't have the car, you don't get the girl. The unspoken threat is that you'll be less if you don't. You'll miss out on enjoyment, prestige, status, or even lose your cool factor.

The House I Bought Without Asking My Wife

Fear of missing out might have cost my marriage. If my sweet wife wasn't as patient and forgiving as she is, she might have ended it with what I'm about to tell you.

Like every city, Orlando has different neighborhoods. When Kathy and I first got married we lived in the attic apartment of a nice, elderly woman's house. It was...um...quaint. You couldn't sit up in bed because you'd hit the roof. It was small, but we loved it. You couldn't beat the price.

Then we bought a house in beautiful Orlo Vista, nestled between Orlando and Lake Buena Vista. Actually, it was an old, wood-frame house I bought from my dad, a fixer upper in an area of town where we didn't let the boys out without Secret Service protection. It was adequate, but we dreamed of the day when we could live in a normal neighborhood. We outgrew that house after ten years, so we went house hunting.

There was this house for sale in another questionable neighborhood. Well, to say the neighborhood was questionable was actually a compliment. Kathy actually rode by and looked at the house and vetoed it with a glance. But I called and talked to the lady who was selling the house. Mrs. Gossman saw me coming a mile away. She was witty and charming, and she could sell ice to penguins in the North Pole. She had a way of making the house look like the deal of the century. Plus, other buyers were interested in it. (So she said.)

One Sunday morning, with my dad in tow—and not Kathy (that's key)—I bought the house. After all, my dad offered to pay the deposit for me. How could I resist? When I told her, my wife was so overwhelmed with emotion that she broke down and cried. I thought it was joy.

We actually lived in that house until the home invasion. I wish I were kidding...

Things are better now. Kathy forgave me, and we now live in a home we actually like surrounded by neighbors we love and trust.

Had I not been so afraid of missing out on the "deal of a lifetime" I could have rested knowing that God would provide the right house at the right time with the right process. FOMO pressures us to take shortcuts that lead us into blind alleys where costly wrong choices are made.

> FOMO pressures us to take shortcuts
> that lead us into blind alleys where
> costly wrong choices are made.

I believe part of the antidote to the fear of missing out is contentment. When you are content with your life you are at peace and much less susceptible to the callings of different fears. Discontentment opens the door to the feelings that having or buying or doing something can make things better, or at least make you feel better.

One of my good friends once lost all of his earthly possessions in a house fire. He later told me that what he found surprising was that he had to think hard to even remember what was in that house. We hold on to things and give them such value. We can worry about losing them and work to build stockpiles of things we value. We fear losing them, but most often, if we do lose them, we just say, "Oh well," and move on. How much better to live freely, without all that stress and energy given to managing needless stuff.

Of course, saying that, I must also confess that Kathy and I do collect stuff. I have a spoon collection, a coffee mug collection, and way too many T-shirts from places I've visited that stuff my dresser drawer. I don't even think about these things until I look at them, and then they become valuable for a split second. Then I move on. While I place value on these mementos, if it all burned up tomorrow I would be just fine.

When? When? When? When, Oh, When?

I spent stress-filled years battling the fear of missing out while I waited for my time to launch.

When I was in my twenties I had a short career as a traveling Christian music artist. I was going to be the next Steven Curtis Chapman (in my mind anyway). I had been working in my parents' appliance store, where I'd worked pretty much all my life up until that point, and it was my time to break out. I told myself I would *never* be back there.

It's not that I had a bad relationship with my parent/bosses; it was actually really good. Still, I remember when I left my job my dad was really angry. Dad did not believe I was right or agree with my decision. He had always hoped I would grow up to take over the family business when he retired.

I launched my music career with great joy and expectation. I had already recorded one album and was working on my second. My main problem was I had a terrible work ethic, and I was not providing well for my family. After a few years my dear friend and pastor recommended that I go and get a real job for a season and allow God to work on my character. I agreed and decided to give up my music for a while. I figured fixing my character would take maybe about four months. *Haha!*

I remember when I made the decision to lay that down, I felt the Spirit of God speak to me these words: "Remember I used Moses after forty years on the backside of the desert." With my tail tucked between my legs I went to my dad and asked for my job back. I thought to myself, "Never say never."

After a while being back at the store I begin to think, "OK, this season must be over by now. It's time for me to get back out on the road." But as I would pray about it, all I ever felt God say was no. In my prayers I would cry out to Him, "Please don't let me miss Your will."

What I thought would be a few months stretched into years. I couldn't believe this was taking so long, and I wondered how soon God would release me back out onto the road. My close friend and spiritual advisor Averill was my sounding board. I would call her and say, "What's going on, and why won't God let me get back into ministry?" She kept drawing my attention back to my wife and kids and said I should just focus on being a good daddy and husband.

All the while in my desperate, stress-filled prayers I would cry out to God, "Please don't let me miss Your will. Please don't let me miss Your will!" I must have prayed that anxious prayer thousands of times. I used to wonder why God kept the desire to minister in my heart and yet would not release me to do so. It didn't make any sense. I would pray, "God, take this desire away from me if You're never going to allow me to do it."

It was the biggest example of FOMO ever. I knew that (or at least I thought that) God had a calling on my life. I loved ministering and sharing my faith in an onstage context. I felt called to it. I had had a measure of success doing it. I felt my life passing, and I felt that I needed to be out there building a singing ministry. Being on permanent hold was driving me crazy.

I'm not the first person who'd tasted ministry and then got placed on the backside of the desert.

Mighty Moses tried to launch himself into his calling when early in his life he saw an Egyptian beating a Hebrew slave. He took matters into his own hands and killed the Egyptian. The next day, he tried to take a leadership role again when he saw two Hebrews arguing, and he tried to break up the argument. They looked at him with disdain and said, "What are you going to do, kill us too?"

He realized that news of what he'd done the day before was getting out, and Pharaoh would be coming after him, so he ran for the hills. Moses spent the next forty years on the backside of the desert working in an appliance store, I mean, tending sheep.

Joseph is my favorite Old Testament character. The account of his life is a grand-scale example of someone who had to defer his plans indefinitely. As a teenager Joseph was the gifted favorite son of his father, Jacob (later renamed Israel), and his eleven jealous brothers hated him for it. Joseph had powerful dreams indicating that he would be some sort of ruler someday, and he wasn't shy about sharing this with his brothers. He told them that in his dream he saw them tying up bundles of grain. Suddenly his bundle stood up tall, and their bundles gathered around and bowed low before his bundle. He told them about another dream in which the sun and moon and eleven stars were bowing low to him.

His brothers hated him with such intensity that they decided to kill him. Ultimately, to avoid the guilt of murder, they sold him into slavery. They put blood all over his cherished coat of many colors and took it to their father, allowing Jacob to believe that Joseph had been eaten by wild animals.

The Lord was with Joseph and blessed the work of his hands. He caused Joseph to prosper in whatever circumstance he found himself. He was taken as a slave to Egypt and purchased by Potiphar, the captain of the guard of Pharaoh. There he spent years as a slave, but he rose quickly to be second only to Potiphar in all his household. After a time he was falsely accused of trying to rape Potiphar's wife, and he was thrown into prison, where he spent even more years.

It sure seems things went from bad to worse for Joseph, and it looked like he got farther and farther away from being any sort of ruler. Yet, each step backward in Joseph's life was an important step that eventually led him to being ruler over all Egypt. He became second in command only behind Pharaoh himself. His long season as a slave and then a prisoner prepared him to rule and was the pathway to the fulfillment of his dream. He learned things as a slave and in prison that he would need as ruler. His experiences in prison led to his promotion.

One day God whispered something to my heart that turned my anxious fear of missing out into a grace-filled peace. I was crying out to Him yet again after years of doing so. "Please don't let me miss Your will, oh, God. Please don't let me miss Your will."

Unexpectedly, He whispered tenderly, "I heard you the first time."

Astonished, I said to myself, "Wait a minute? Lord, You mean You've got this?"

It hit me like a freight train: God, who made ears, can surely hear me. God, who made eyes, can see me and knows exactly where I am.

He who guides the birds to their food and planets to their appointed orbit can surely guide me to my heart's desire. Suddenly I realized that all that stress I'd been carrying about missing out on what God had for my life was totally unnecessary. Beyond that, it was a lack of trust. Matthew 6 flowed into my mind: "Don't worry about anything" (author's paraphrase).

If God knows the number of the very hairs on my head, and He is intimately acquainted with all my ways—indeed, if He is living in me and He knows my very thoughts—then how can He not know the things I'm so very concerned about? What an "aha!" moment! All that stress and anxiety—gone! I sighed deeply as my shoulders dropped and the weight lifted, and I smiled.

I felt like I needed the plan. I needed to know the itinerary.

> *Look at the birds of the air; they do not sow or reap or store away in barns, and yet your heavenly Father feeds them. Are you not much more valuable than they? Can any one of you by worrying add a single hour to your life?*
> —Matthew 6:26–27, NIV

If I want to see the fulfillment of my heart's desire in God, I do have a role to play. There is something I need to be doing, but it's not worry. It's simply to abide in Jesus.

> *I am the vine, you are the branches. He who abides in Me, and I in him, bears much fruit; for without Me you can do nothing. If anyone does not abide in Me, he is cast out as a branch and is withered; and they gather them and throw them into the fire, and they are burned. If you abide in Me, and My words*

abide in you, you will ask what you desire, and
it shall be done for you.

—JOHN 15:5–7

So, I don't, you don't, we don't ever have to fear missing out if we are staying close to Him, abiding.

I quit stressing about it and began to pray much differently: "God, I trust You with my heart's desire, and I leave it in Your capable hands." I sighed, "Ahhh…" Much better. "Lord, if and when You want me to do something, I trust that You will make sure I know where to be and what to do."

Delight yourself in the LORD, and he will give
you the desires of your heart.

—PSALM 37:4, ESV

It is profound how much more peace and joy I began to experience just trusting God instead of carrying that burden myself. I began to use the time I had spent worrying about what I was supposed to do to instead serve others. I became less self-centered. What a relief.

When Moses took matters into his own hands it turned him toward the desert. When Joseph bragged to his brothers, they sold him into slavery. Joseph and his brothers were reunited later in the story in one of the greatest acts of forgiveness ever recorded. There is a key in what Joseph told his brothers: "You meant it for evil, but God meant it for good" (Gen. 50:20, author's paraphrase).

God used Moses's desert experience to shape him into the leader he would become. God used Joseph's slavery, and God is working in our lives too.

God knew all along that He was going to turn me into a passionate, burning Bush. But the fear of missing out could easily have caused me to act on my own and out of God's timing instead of waiting.

It could have easily moved me to trust my own anxious thoughts and impulsive actions instead of God. We humans tend to be short sighted. We think in moments. God thinks with eternity in mind.

When a baby chick develops it is protected in the egg. God keeps us protected in His loving care while our dreams and calling are getting ready to hatch. When it approaches the time to hatch, the chick has to peck at the shell with all its might to break out. If we opened an egg at this point the chick wouldn't have the strength to survive the outside world. As the chick struggles to emerge, it gets stronger and stronger until it breaks free. That is what the preparation process is like. We think we are missing out on all the things in our heart, but we are really being prepared to launch into the amazing life God has for us.

> **We think we are missing out on all the things in our heart, but we are really being prepared to launch into the amazing life God has for us.**

We can shorten or lengthen the process by our obedience or disobedience, but we must all go through the process. It is about a three- to five-day journey from Egypt to the Promised Land, yet because of their disobedience and grumbling the Israelites spent forty years wandering around in the desert. They had to go through the desert. We all do. But because of their attitude about it, their time in the desert was greatly increased.

We can see the folly now, but they actually longed to be back in Egypt, in slavery. They wanted the things of the familiar world rather than the things of God because they feared missing out. They didn't trust God, so they romanticized their past slavery, actually longing for it.

In the beginning I was so discontent. All I did was grumble and complain. I was like a five-year-old kid in the backseat of the car. "Are we there yet? Are we there yet?"

We are given the privilege of peace and contentment now if we just realize a few things.

In Luke's Gospel, Jesus sent His apostles and seventy-two other chosen disciples out to go into the cities where Jesus Himself would be going, instructing them not to take even a change of clothing or an extra pair of shoes. He instructed them to go and heal the sick, cast out demons, and preach the Good News, accepting whatever hospitality was shown them. They were simply to trust God for their provision. When they returned rejoicing in all the miracles, Jesus said, "Do not rejoice in this, that the spirits are subject to you, but rather rejoice because your names are written in heaven" (Luke 10:20).

When we get our contentment from being His child, see the amazing privilege and hope in calling God our Father, and find our delight in Him rather than worldly things, then the Scriptures promise that He will give us the desires of our heart. God wants us to place our trust in Him. When we do that, He in turn gives us His peace and joy. It isn't easy or automatic, and our tendency is to take that trust back from Him. But as we learn to trust Him more and more we find that joy and peace will become more and more the place we live.

Add to that, Christians have a promised future in heaven, where joy shall never end; every tear will be wiped away; where there will be no sorrow or suffering, no disease or sickness; and most importantly, where we will live with Jesus in His glorious presence evermore! This is just a tiny glimpse of what awaits us. In heaven we will receive a new, glorified, eternal body, free from sin and sickness! The Book of First Corinthians chapter 15 describes this new body by comparing a tiny seed to a mighty tree. Perhaps you've heard this spoken at funerals: "Mortality will put on immortality, corruptible will put on incorruptible" (v. 53, author's paraphrase).

Having an attitude of gratitude and keeping the reality of our future in heaven in mind will keep us from fearing that we are missing out and keep us from chasing things that will not last anyhow.

The enemy will tempt us with the counterfeit so that we miss out on the genuine. He will keep us building a house of cards so that we miss out on the home God has for us in heaven.

> *In my Father's house are many rooms. If it were not so, would I have told you that I go to prepare a place for you? And if I go and prepare a place for you, I will come again and will take you to myself, that where I am you may be also.*
> —JOHN 14:2–3, ESV

Fear overvalues worthless, worldly trinkets and attractions and devalues the things of God that are of eternal worth.

The only thing we should fear missing out on is God's best for us now and for eternity.

Success looks different to God than it does to us. After Moses went to Pharaoh the first time, Pharaoh didn't let God's people go. Quite the opposite. He made life much harder for them. Moses was a success in that he obediently did what God told him to do, but Moses didn't feel much like a success.

Success looks different to God than it does to us.

Sometimes success needs a different definition. God is looking for obedient devotion. The results are in His court. The battle between Moses and Pharaoh had just begun; Moses just didn't know it was a ten-round fight.

When someone first suggested I become a George W. Bush impersonator, I did not warm up to the idea. In fact, I downright refused even to consider it. I couldn't even imagine it being a good thing because I didn't want to miss out on being a pastor or a singer/songwriter. Surely God wouldn't want me to stoop to this. I mean, after all these years waiting, trusting Him...an impersonator?

Ever have a thought just stop you in your tracks? I did. In the midst of this refusal to even consider it, I heard a question: How do you know it's not God?

That question changed my life. Once I opened up to the idea that God could be behind this crazy career choice, I started to pray about it. When I did that, I knew in my heart that He was leading me to become a George W. Bush impersonator. What I thought would be a disaster has been a phenomenal success. That's the way it is when you follow God rather than your fear of missing out.

The best way to combat FOMO is by being all in with God. Once you've decided, acknowledged, and committed to the fact that God is always right and you can always trust Him no matter what, all you ever need to know is which way He is leading you. Once you know that, there is no second guessing, because God is always right. Once I prayed and sensed God's direction, the decision was automatically made in my heart. No fear or doubt deterred me. There's no safer or better place to put your trust. God is your refuge, your protector, and your tower of strength.

> *Do not fear, for I am with you; Do not anxiously look about you, for I am your God. I will strengthen you, surely I will help you.*
> —ISAIAH 41:10, NASU

CHAPTER 10

The Sum of All Fear

When I heard that my friend Marvin had been diagnosed with Hepatitis C, I felt so sorry for him and his family. I had no real-life experience with caring for someone who was really sick. I also wondered what it must be like to be him or his wife. I knew very little about the illness, just that it was life-threatening and could be transferred. The whole thing scared me. I couldn't fathom going through their trial, because it wasn't my trial—until it was.

I'll never forget the unique wave of fear that hit my wife and me the second our friend and family doctor pronounced the test results: "Kathy, you've tested positive for Hepatitis C." Liver transplants and life-threatening treatments were apparently in our future. I remember the thought process Kathy and I went through immediately after that fateful moment. Apparently she had contracted it from a blood transfusion twenty or so years prior during the birth of our first son.

As we left the doctor's office Kathy asked me if she could just walk a while and be alone with her thoughts. While I waited in the car she walked and prayed, "God help me understand what just happened. How am I supposed to deal with this? How will I carry on each day?" Kathy wanted to just drop into depression. But then, she didn't want to. She had kids and grandkids to love on. She needed to be strong for them as long as she could. As she walked she reconciled that no one knows the hour of our death anyways, and no one is promised a particular number of years. When she returned to the car she said with a halfhearted smile, "I could walk out into that street and get hit by a car today. Nobody knows when they'll die. I trust God. Let's go."

> *The Lord gave, and the Lord has taken away;*
> *Blessed be the name of the Lord.*
> —Job 1:21

Kathy's situation went from bad to worse, and even the hope of treatment was taken away. We were basically told to go home and hope a better treatment would someday be developed. Eight long years we struggled through procedures, biopsies, diet changes, crazy alternative treatments, blood tests, sonograms, and more tests, all with no real change.

To those not looking closely enough, through it all, Kathy seemed normal. Her joy was there. Her zeal for life and adventure were all fine. She would simply absorb each round of bad or good news, give it to God, and go on. She was a genuine example of the grace of God, full of laughter and service to others.

Although the Lord truly strengthened Kathy, when she was alone she spent many hours crying over what she thought would be her soon departure from this life. She cried because she thought of how much she would miss her children. Kathy, who loves others so much, cried at the thought of not seeing her precious grandchildren grow up. Through the tears she always kept her trust in the living God, and she held on to hope and God's grace.

As for me, I tried my best to serve her and support her. I received grace too. I received the grace to be there for her and to try and represent hope and love and just be an ear to listen when Kathy needed me. I wrestled with my own fears of contracting the disease by placing my trust in God. God's grace was there when we needed it. Kathy says I stepped up and served her with kindness and thoughtfulness. Even I can be transformed by grace.

Every holiday that passed, although she hoped it wouldn't be true, Kathy feared that it would be her last—her last Easter, last Christmas, last birthday. Every new ache and pain was accompanied by fear. We received much help from the writings of Randy Alcorn, founder of Eternal Perspective Ministries, which I heartily recommend. Randy wrote the book *Heaven*, which gave us so much hope about our eternal future. Just knowing that her future in heaven would be so wonderful gave Kathy much hope. It still does.

About a year ago Kathy's liver doctor told us about a new treatment she might qualify for. We held out little hope because we had heard that so many times before. A new drug claimed to cure people of Hepatitis C with little or no side effects. This was profound because the previous treatment was at times worse than the disease itself and actually had killed many people.

At long last, Kathy qualified for a treatment! She simply took one pill a day for twelve weeks. Simple. She experienced no side effects at all. We were celebrating our thirty-third wedding anniversary standing in the middle of a department store when we got the phone call with the test results. No more Hepatitis C! She's totally cured! We both screamed! And cried! And hugged! And bought clothes.

Although for most of us the vast majority of the things we fear never come about, we all do still die eventually. I believe that death is just a change of venue. For the believer, going to heaven is like going from the cheesy preshow at an amusement park into a 3-D, total immersion experience! Only it isn't a show. It isn't a dream. It's real!

> *O death, where is your victory? O death, where is your sting?*
> —1 CORINTHIANS 15:55, NASU

I believe that God created heaven as a place to dwell with Him for eternity, enjoying mega bliss forever. Jesus prayed, "Father, I desire that they also whom You gave Me may be with Me where I am" (John 17:24).

If you are in God and abiding in Him, you have no need to fear anything. If you must endure some pain in this life, God wants to give you all the grace you need to handle it. You can have just what you need, just when you need it. That's the nature of God's grace; it goes where it's needed. Kathy let fear predict her early demise, causing her so much sadness, as she fearfully anticipated her death. Yet, God had other plans. The disease is gone, and Kathy is able to give loving support and hope to others who are in need.

If we live only for this life it may be that this life is all we will ever enjoy.

We are children of God, and heaven is our eternal home. If you are a Christian, that is just a fact. This world, with all its temporal fascination, is passing away. We are of a different place. If we live only for this life it may be that this life is all we will ever enjoy.

> *Do not love the world or the things in the world. If anyone loves the world, the love of*

the Father is not in him. For all that is in the world—the lust of the flesh, the lust of the eyes, and the pride of life—is not of the Father but is of the world. And the world is passing away, and the lust of it; but he who does the will of God abides forever.
— 1 JOHN 2:15–17

Fear of dying is associated with fear of the unknown. Loving God and learning about and treasuring heaven is the best antidote. I long for that heavenly city. I long to be in my glorified body, where I will *never* sin again, *never* die again, *never* be sick, sad, or suffer ever again. But mostly I long to physically embrace Jesus and tell Him face to face how much I love Him. I long to look into His eyes as He tells me how much He loves me.

If all this God stuff sounds like Greek to you, it may be that you've never been introduced to your gracious, forgiving heavenly Father.

For God so loved the world that He gave His only begotten Son, that whoever believes in Him should not perish but have everlasting life.
—JOHN 3:16

The Bible is loaded with promises for those that follow God. Jesus made a relationship with God possible. Yes, a real fear-destroying relationship with God is available for anyone who will come to Him in humility. Jesus came to the earth for the direct purpose of paying the price of our sins so that we can be forgiven.

No one merits heaven on their own; it is a gift from God. God's arms are outstretched, waiting to receive you, forgive you, and give you eternal life.

The bottom line reason we fear death is the fear of punishment after death. If you don't have the assurance of a relationship with God and the peace of having been forgiven for all your wrongdoings, why not ask God to forgive you right now and give Him your life? If you do that from your heart, He will forgive you and give you eternal life.

The Bible serves up warnings as well as promises of reward. We are invited into a loving relationship with our heavenly Father, but we are also warned that if we refuse this offer of eternal life, then eternal punishment awaits. Yes, if you don't have a relationship with God, fearing death is very appropriate.

Hell is meant to be a deterrent. It is meant to drive you toward God. Apart from God, fear is appropriate. Without the forgiveness of your sins, hell awaits you, and it is more awful than you can imagine.

But God is kind, merciful, forgiving, perfect love, generous, patient and gracious. He is the best friend of millions of Christians around the world. He is also the Creator, righteous and holy, perfect and pure. He openly invites all who will come to enter by first receiving His free gift of forgiveness for our sins against Him.

> *For all have sinned and fall short of the glory of God, being justified ["as a gift," NASU] freely by His grace through the redemption that is in Christ Jesus.*
> —ROMANS 3:23–24

God the Father accepted the sacrifice of Jesus the Son as a substitute for us. He took our place so that we could be forgiven. What love!

Jesus gave Himself to ransom us, and His blood cleanses us from all unrighteousness.

Each of us has a remarkable invitation to become a part of God's holy family, an adopted, forgiven child. But first we must acknowledge the fact that we have broken God's laws, express sorrow, and then turn from breaking them again. (This is called repentance.) We must ask God for forgiveness, accepting Jesus's death on the cross as our substitute, asking Jesus to come into our hearts to become our own Lord.

Here is a good prayer you can pray to give your life to Jesus and be cleansed and forgiven of your sin. Pray this prayer to God if you are ready to give Him your life. You can say:

> *Dear Jesus, I'm so sorry for my sins. Please forgive me. Thank You for dying on the cross in my place, taking the punishment I deserve. Thank You. Please come into my heart and be my Lord, my Savior. Jesus, I give You my life. Please help me to live in a way that pleases You. Amen.*

Or you can simply pray from your own heart. Just tell Him you're sorry for your sins, ask Him to forgive you, and ask Him to come into your heart to live forever. Give Him control of your life, and you will begin a new life in Him!

If you said a prayer from your heart, turned from your sins, and honestly gave your life to Jesus, your sins are now forever taken away from you, forever forgiven. Congratulations! Now you are His child, and you will forever live with Him in His glorious kingdom.

The Bible tells us that when you receive God's gift of forgiveness and new life in Jesus, Jesus Himself becomes one with you. He now lives in you and will walk with you for the rest of your life. Great, great news indeed!

Please start reading the Bible right away to get to know the Lord. I recommend beginning with the Gospel of John. It is fascinating reading, and I believe you will love it. There are also lots of great Bible apps you can download onto your phone. The one I use is called YouVersion, and it offers reading plans with an audio feature so you can just listen as well as read. As you read and listen your faith will rise, and faith conquers fear.

Welcome to the life of an overcomer. Welcome to a more fearless life!

Nobody wants to face a life-threatening illness. But wouldn't it be amazing to be able to face life unafraid and with a great outlook, no matter what your present or future holds? I've seen folks face extreme difficulty with peace and joy, even in extreme pain.

The apostle Paul had to deal with a persistent affliction he called his thorn in the flesh. He asked God to remove it:

> *But he said to me, "My grace is sufficient for you, for my power is made perfect in weakness." Therefore I will boast all the more gladly about my weaknesses, so that Christ's power may rest on me.*
> —2 CORINTHIANS 12:9, NIV

Yes, I do know that God gives His children grace to handle whatever difficulties come our way. I have seen this over and over again in the lives of loved ones who have suffered devastating illnesses and calamities. God didn't give me Marvin's grace. That's why I couldn't fathom his situation. My grace to overcome fear came when I needed it, and if you believe in Jesus, yours will too.

Incidentally, my friend just returned from snow skiing in Dubai. He is also now totally Hep C free.

Conclusion

For God has not given us a spirit of fear, but of power and of love and of a sound mind.
—2 TIMOTHY 1:7, AUTHOR'S PARAPHRASE

The thief comes only to steal and kill and destroy; I have come that they may have life, and have it to the full.
—JOHN 10:10, NIV

Faith is *real!* Fear is a phantom!
Faith is *substance!* Fear is a fake!
Faith is *truthful!* Fear is phony!
Faith is *fearless!* Fear is faithless!

The tempter uses fear to try to convince us that God is not faithful, that God's motives are suspect. He uses fear to argue against God's loving commands in order to rob us of the blessing that comes from being obedient children of God. Fear wants to be your lord and master.

The basic goal of all these internal arguments is to keep you from stepping out in faith; from being courageous, obedient, bold, and faithful; and from doing what is right.

Now that we know our enemy, we know that it can be defeated. We now know that fear is a deception, an evil illusion designed to keep us from fulfilling our dreams and maximizing our potential. We can fearlessly launch those dreams, start those ventures, and resolve those relationships. Your fearless adventures will transform you and transform the world!

We not only know how to fight; we are fighting and winning the War on Fear. We are a band of brothers and sisters. We are enlisted in the battle together. We are not in this alone. We have God, we have truth, and we have each other.

I can't know what small and great things you will accomplish with your fearless life, but I know this: the world will be grateful that you live, that you love, and that you act courageously.

We are beacons meant to shine. We are invited to thrive, to fully and fearlessly live that abundant life. Make it your daily declaration that you are going to live free from fear, and show others how to do the same. Shout the truth from the rooftops!

Notes

Introduction
1. Jack Canfield, quoted at http://www.goodreads.com/
quotes/495741-everything-you-want-is-on-the-other-side-of-fear
(accessed September 7, 2016).

Chapter 1: What Is Fear?
1. *Mr. Magorium's Wonder Emporium*, written and directed by
Zach Helm (2007; Los Angeles, CA: Twentieth Century Fox Home
Entertainment, 2008), DVD.

Chapter 3: The Dream Killer
1. Billy Joe Daughtery, "Don't Give Up," Victory Christian
Center, April 5, 2009.

Chapter 4: The Nature of Fear
1. See Etienne Benson, "The Synaptic Self," *American
Psychological Association* 33 (Nov. 2002): 40, http://www.apa.org/
monitor/nov02/synaptic.aspx (accessed September 7, 2016).
2. Kerry J. Ressler, "MDMA, Used in Treatment for PTSD,
Helps Reduce Fear Response in Mice," *Brain & Behavior
Research Foundation*, available at https://bbrfoundation.org/
brain-matters-discoveries/mdma-used-in-treatment-for-ptsd-helps-
reduce-fear-response-in-mice (accessed September 7, 2016).

Chapter 5: Fear of Terror

1. *Merriam-Webster.com* (2011), s.v. "terror," accessed August 27, 2016.

2. The phrase "future grace" comes from the book *Future Grace* by John Piper (Colorado Springs, CO: Multnomah, 2005).

3. Metro Life Church Celebration Conference, High Springs, FL, October 2001. A link to Terry's message is available at www. WarOnFearBook.com.

Chapter 6: Fear of Insignificance

1. Robert S. McGee, *The Search for Significance* (Nashville, TN: Thomas Nelson, 2003), 88.

Chapter 7: Fear of Man (or Woman)

1. Videos of Odell Beckham Jr.'s pregame practice and catch may be seen at https://www.youtube.com/watch?v=Qw9B_JMkLZ8 and https://www.youtube.com/watch?v=zxbz3DDQzHU.

2. Stephen Mansfield, *The Faith of George W. Bush* (Lake Mary, FL: Charisma House, 2004).

Chapter 8: Fear of Public Speaking

1. A video of my performance at the Comedy and Magic Club is available at www.WarOnFearBook.com.

Chapter 9: Fear of Missing Out

1. Jerry Seinfeld, *I'm Telling You for the Last Time—Live on Broadway* (1998; New York, NY: HBO Home Video, 1999), DVD.

About the Author

John Morgan's world-famous impersonation of George W. Bush has generated billions of laughs from millions of astonished people. John combines comedy with passionate inspiration to deliver powerful and unique speaking presentations. In the same way, John writes with a passion and authenticity that make his written messages life changing.

John and his wife, Kathy, live in sunny Orlando, Florida. They enjoy a close relationship with their four adult sons and their families. John travels internationally as an inspirational speaker, comedian, and George W. Bush impersonator. John's passion is to motivate people toward personal freedom, spiritual health, and professional success.

Contact the Author

Please visit www.JohnCMorgan.com or www.WarOnFearBook. com for more information about John Morgan's work as a speaker, impersonator, and author. Keep up with him at his blog, www. JohnMorgan.tv.

To have John deliver this message or other passionate, live presentations to your church, association, or corporation, please contact him at info@johncmorgan.com.

Follow him on Facebook at John C. Morgan, on Twitter (@ BushGuy), or on Instagram (@BushGuy43).